A MOTIVE FOR MURDER

A MOTIVE FOR MURDER

A MOTIVE FOR MURDER

Copies of Raymond D. Mason's books may be ordered by contacting (see list in the back of the book)

www.CreateSpace.com

Or

www.amazon.com

Or

For personally autographed copies:

RMason3092@aol.com

Book Cover by Raymond D. Mason

Photograph provided by Michael Hawk Photography

Printed in the United States

CHAPTER

1

THE ICE CUBES wrapped in the damp bar towel felt good against the cut lip I'd suffered at the hands of the irate victim of my off colored barb. The woman's fingertips gently rubbing my temples felt even better, as I lay flat on my back on the floor with my head resting comfortably in her lap formed by her kneeling position.

"Someday Harley you will learn that not everyone possess the same sense of humor that you do," the woman that also happened to be my fiancé, Cassandra Roberts, said softly, but in a serious tone of voice.

"Yeah, but then I wouldn't get to lay here like this, Cass," I said, wincing a bit as I tried to smile. "What'd that guy hit me with anyway, a crowbar?"

"I think the technical term for it is 'fist.' You know what that is, don't you Harley? That's what you make when you curl your fingers in towards the palms of your hands and squeeze. You should know the term by now; seeing as how you've been the recipient of so many of them lately," Cassandra said as she demonstrated how a person makes a fist.

"Oh, yeah, I think I have heard that term before; along with, dukes and mitts. Is that sorehead gone now?"

"Yes, Harley, he's gone."

"Well, in that case, help me up," I said as I moved to an upright position.

Joe Gladstone, the owner/bartender, looked over the bar and shook his head, "You okay, Quinn?" he asked.

"No problem, Joe. Who was that masked man, anyway?"

"Sergeant Gonzales of the Seattle PD; you're lucky he was in a good mood," Joe laughed.

"Yeah, well he's lucky I was in a good mood; otherwise he might have killed me," I said as Cassandra helped me to my feet.

"I would have been worried, Harley but I've seen you in that position so many times now, I almost don't recognize you when you're standing or sitting; sitting anywhere other than the floor that is," Joe went on.

"Give me another JD straight up; and a fresh ice cube," I ordered.

"Coming right up," Joe said and then turned and limped down the long, narrow rubber mat that ran the length of the bar well.

Joe had been a motorcycle cop with the SPD until he was forced to retire from the force due to a bad spill he had taken while pursuing a carjacker that decided he didn't want to be caught. I caught the punk, however, and if he's still walking at all, you can bet his limp is worse than Joe's. Of course that was before I was married to Mary Jane and Jack Daniels had become my best friend. I'd been able to divorce Mary Jane, but Jack was too hard to lose.

Cassandra Roberts, the woman in my life, had been my fiancé for five years and the best friend a guy could have. She'd tried to help me kick Jack D. out of my life, but he kept hanging around. Lately he was trying to take a little more control of me. He would own me if it wasn't for Cass.

Cassandra had the greenest eyes I'd ever seen on a human being. You see them on cats, but never humans. She stood a shade over five feet tall and weighed about a hundred five pounds, but she was one hundred percent woman. She had medium length hair that was so blond it looked bleached, but it was as natural as she was. Her skin was a light tan the year round, thanks to her mother who was half-Cherokee. It was as soft and smooth as fine velvet. She was easy going, but don't make her mad.

"I think we should go after this, Harley. You've got a client to meet with in the morning and I have to go to work, remember," Cass said as she brushed my cheek with the back of her fingers.

I turned and looked at her through bleary, bloodshot eyes and tried to smile with my split lip. She was right; I had forgotten that I had to meet with a prospective client since it had been so long since I'd had one.

"You want to look your best so you'll make a good impression on him," Cass said as she looked at me almost pitiful.

I must have looked a mess; a real loser; a drunk. I pulled myself straight up on the bar stool and straightened my tie and tried to make myself look sober.

"Yes, I have to meet with Rodney Philpot, the big man around Seattle," I said with a slur.

Just then Joe returned with my shot of JD and set in front of me. Cass laid a twenty on the bar that Joe picked up, but continued to look hard at me.

"You driving, Cass," Joe asked?

"No, Joe, I'm going to let Harley drive," Cass said sarcastically then added with a smile, "of course I am."

"He's cut off for the night here," Joe said and turned and walked away.

I downed my shot just as Joe returned with Cass's change. I looked at him through heavy lidded eyes that swimmingly saw one and a half of him. I smiled happily as Cass helped me off the barstool. I vaguely remember singing, "Show me the way to go home, I'm tired and I want to go to bed," as we left the bar with the name the 911 Club, which was also the bar's address.

Cass got me to my car and drove me to my three room apartment on Fairview Avenue. She got me upstairs and into my flat, got me ready for bed, set my alarm clock, tucked me into bed; kissed me goodnight and left. I vaguely remember hearing the front door close.

The sound of the alarm clock jolted me out of my stupefied dream world where nothing made any sense. My eyelids felt like they had sandpaper on the insides and the clanging alarm didn't do a thing for my throbbing head and swollen lip.

I managed to shut the alarm off after knocking it off the nightstand and retrieving it by the electrical cord. I lay in bed for several seconds trying to remember why anyone would set the alarm on my clock. Finally the reason fought its way through the whiskey soaked recesses of my brain allowing me to remember that I was to meet with a prospective client.

I needed coffee and a lot of it. Maybe a shower would help. I touched my busted lip and tried to recall the events that led up to me being introduced to someone's fist. Like the old saying goes, "I hope I had a good time last night because my head hurts and I can't remember a thing." Well, if it isn't an old saying, it should be.

The water cascading over my head and down my body felt so good I didn't want to get out of the shower. I stood with my hands against the wall and my eyes closed for at least five minutes without moving. When the hot water started to cool, however, I hurriedly lathered up and got out before all the hot water was gone. The shower made me feel somewhat better.

By the time I'd showered the coffee was finished brewing and I managed to take a sip around the sore spot on my lip. I hate myself on the mornings after like this. I've kicked Jack out of my life fifty times on mornings like these, but the jerk keeps coming back. Maybe this time...no, who am I kidding.

I shaved and dressed, sipping my coffee every so often to get some caffeine in me so it could do its part in preparing me for my meeting. By the time I'd finished I looked halfway presentable. Now a little breakfast and I'd feel like a hundred bucks; green and wrinkled.

The toast hung up in the toaster, sending up a gray smoke signal, but I managed to salvage it while avoiding electrical shock by using a plastic fork. The orange juice was the only thing in my refrigerator that hadn't exceeded the 'use by' date and after splashing a little Grey Goose Vodka in it, tasted really fresh. Someday I'll have to try OJ straight; I'll bet it would be good.

The phone rang just as I'd polished off my toast and blackberry jam and I grabbed it up while licking my fingers.

"Quinn, here," halfway expecting a telemarketer of some kind; either live or a recording.

"I see you're up. I'm very proud of you," the silky smooth voice said on the other end. It was my Cassandra.

"Of course I'm up. I have a very important meeting at eleven o'clock, remember?"

"Ten, Harley. The appointment's at ten," Cassandra said slowly. I could just imagine the look on her face.

"I know it, I was just teasing you," I lied. Actually I couldn't remember when the appointment was; mainly because I knew Cass would tell me.

"Yeah, right; are you all dressed and ready to make a good impression...I hope?" Cass said sounding almost like a mother.

"Yes Mommy Dearest," I teased.

She hates that term.

"I'm not your mother and I pity the poor woman that had to raise you up. She should be given the highest award a civilian can get for bravery and going above and beyond the call of duty," Cass rattled off.

"Don't get your girdle in a bind, honey; I was just yanking your chain," I laughed. Wincing from the lip I added quickly, "Hey, how'd I get this split lip, anyway? Did you do it?"

"Your mouth got it for you, don't you remember. Sgt. Gonzales of the SPD popped you for your jab at 'wetbacks,' as you called them."

"What does he look like this morning?" I asked.

"The same as yesterday morning, but with a swollen fist, I'd imagine."

"Oh...did I swing at him?"

"No, Harley. Two things landed; his fist landed on your mouth and your butt landed on the floor."

"How long was I out this time?"

"You did better this time, Hon; you were only out for maybe two minutes."

"Ha, ha...made of granite," I exclaimed.

"Yeah, crushed and sifted," Cass corrected. "Well, I've got to get back to work. I just wanted to make sure you were up and around."

"I'll call you after the meeting and let you know what happened. Hopefully I'll have an increase in my income for awhile."

"Hopefully, sweetie; I'll talk to you later; bye, bye."

"Bye, baby; I love you."

"Me too," Cass said and hung up.

RODNEY PHILPOT was a well known and highly respected land developer in and around the Seattle area. His face and/or name appeared on the newspaper society pages so much he was the envy of every state and local politician that ever held, or hoped, to hold office. His wife, Karenna, was an ex-Miss something or other, from a well-to-do family from the East coast. The two of them made a handsome couple.

Philpot's office took up the entire top floor of the six story office building that carried his name. His secretary asked me to have a seat and she'd let Philpot know I was there. As I picked up a magazine and took a seat in a very comfortable half round chair with a low back, she buzzed Philpot. I couldn't hear his end of the conversation, but I assumed he told her it would be a few minutes before he could see me.

"Mr. Philpot will be right with you, Mr. Quinn. Please make yourself comfortable. Would you care for something to drink," she asked pleasantly.

A question like that to an alcoholic is like saying 'Toro' to a Mexican bull. It was all I could do to keep from asking for a Vodka Collins or a shot of Jack. I was able to hold my tongue, however, and heard myself say, "Coffee, black, thank you."

The cute little brunette got up and poured me a cup of coffee and brought it over to me. She was dressed very neatly and seemed very sincere with her smile and remarks.

"That's a very pretty tie, you have on Mr. Quinn. Do you mind if I ask you where you bought it? I'd like to get one for my boyfriend," she purred.

"What, this old thing. Actually I don't know where I got it; I think it was a gift from my fiancé. She buys most of my clothes," I smiled.

The secretary laughed at my honesty and went back behind her desk where she stuck some dictation earphones into her ears and began typing on her desktop keyboard. The staccato sound of her fingers dancing across the keys told me she could type at least sixty five to seventy words a minute. That's about what I type also; but fifty to sixty words would be misspelled.

After about five minutes the door to Philpot's office opened and a tall, thin man with graying hair emerged along with the man I recognized instantly as Rodney Philpot. The tall man looked in my direction and his grey eyes seemed to look right through me. He didn't acknowledge me in any way, although I nodded towards him. His expression told me he was not real happy about the outcome of the meeting he'd had with Philpot.

Rodney Philpot was a tall man, himself; standing around six-foot three or four and weighing two hundred ten to fifteen pounds. His hair was neatly styled and he wore a Western dress suit sans coat. He was well tanned and looked like a picture of health. When he smiled I noticed his pure white, even teeth. He made me feel frumpy.

"I'll be in touch with you, Mr. Poindexter. I hope our next meeting will be a little more amiable," Philpot said evenly flashing a well practiced smile. Mr. Poindexter did not return the smile.

"I hope we can work this thing out Philpot. I've got a lot riding on it. I'll..." Poindexter stopped in mid-sentence and looked my way. After a substantial pause he continued, "Uh, I'll be in the city next Monday. We could talk then."

"Monday will be fine; say eleven o'clock?"

Poindexter nodded his approval and cast another glance in my direction. I couldn't tell if the man was trying to place me from somewhere or was nervous about my over hearing their conversation.

"Marcia, make a note of that, please; eleven o'clock Monday, meeting with Mr. Poindexter. Well, until then Argus take care," Philpot said as he extended his hand towards Poindexter.

The two men shook hands and Poindexter turned for the elevator door as Philpot looked in my direction. The developer started towards me when Poindexter suddenly stopped and looked back at me again.

"Quinn...Sgt. Harley Quinn. I thought that was you," Poindexter said almost spitting the words out of his mouth.

"I beg your pardon," I replied, hoping this wasn't someone else I'd insulted while under JD's influence.

"You busted my son on a DUI about eight years ago. I got it thrown out of court. Argus Poindexter's the name; remember me?" the elderly man snapped.

"Oh yes, I do remember you; vaguely anyway," I said recalling the arrogance the man had displayed after getting the judge to toss the case out of court.

"I hear you got bounced off the force. Something about a little drinking problem you had if memory serves me correctly, is that right," Poindexter said, smiling for the first time?

I felt my temperature rising as I fought the urge to rip into him with a line of expletives that would embarrass him and lose me a possible client. I held my tongue and glanced at Philpot and the secretary who were both staring at me to see how I was going to respond.

"Yes, I retired from the force and have the pension to prove it. I guess you could say that I was able to spot your son easily enough since one drunk relates well to another. By the way, how is your son doing these days?" I said, chewing at the words as I spoke them.

Poindexter stiffened when I asked about his son. His angry demeanor slowly diminished as my words hit an invisible target that I didn't know was there.

He dropped his gaze towards the floor as he said quietly, "He was killed in a car wreck."

When Poindexter said what he did it jogged my memory. I did recall reading about Argus Poindexter Jr. getting killed in a head on collision with a big rig due to his being drunk out of his mind. It had happened about two years after the court incident. Unfortunately the trucker was also killed in the accident.

Poindexter turned around and walked to the elevator stoop shouldered; a portrait of a broken man. I watched him and felt a kind of sadness for the man. Philpot's voice broke into my thoughts.

Mr. Quinn...Rod Philpot; glad to meet you," Philpot said as he moved towards me with his hand extended.

Usually when someone extends a hand towards me there's something in it that hurts, even if it's just a closed fist. I fought off the urge to duck and took Philpot's hand. He had a good, strong grip; not the usual dead fish kind that society types usually have.

I had almost thought the call to my one room, one person office in Seattle's low rent section, was a joke, when I'd gotten it; until I checked the phone's caller ID and checked the number against the number in the phone book. I still didn't know why someone of Philpot's stature in the community would want to hire a washed up ex-cop that specializes in surveillances or divorce cases. I was about to find out.

CHAPTER

2

PHILPOT showed me into his office and told me to have a seat. I set on a divan against a wall that was opposite the full length picture window of which his desk sat in front. The view was beautiful looking out towards Waterfront Park and across Puget Sound and the town of Bremerton. A little different view than the one from my office, you can be sure.

His desk was large enough to play croquette on, but obviously lacked the wickets. It was made of oak and highly polished. The carpet was a powder blue and uniquely decorated with the initials RP, but so small you wouldn't even notice if you didn't look very closely.

Philpot was not one to mince words; he came right to the point of our meeting.

"Mr. Quinn, I need your help."

I looked around the office, "You...need my help; why?"

"I don't know if you know this or not because it's been kept out of the papers up to now, but..."

I didn't let him finish what he was about to say, "Mr. Philpot, excuse me, but do you know who I am?" I asked seriously.

"Yes, I know who you are and I know all about why you were let go from the SPD. The Seattle Chief of Police filled me in completely on you and then highly recommended you to me, along with a strong warning. Keep you off the booze," Philpot said not blinking an eye.

"And you still wanted to talk to me; why?"

"As I was about to tell you when you interrupted, the press has not uncovered the true identify of a derelict who's body was found recently. The police have determined it was murder, but are not about to, and I quote, 'spend much time trying to solve the crime of some wine-o getting killed over a bottle of Muscatel,' end quote. Chief Wells said you would be the perfect man for this job," Philpot explained, not pulling his punches or his words.

I thought for a second, "Because I'm a lush he thinks I'd fit right in with the skid row crowd, is that it?"

Philpot shook his head, "No, no, he didn't mean it that way. He went on to say you were one of the best detectives on the force. From street cop to detective in five years was quite a fete in his eyes. He said you could have been the top investigator in the country, but for your taste for alcohol. No, he meant that you would see and hear things that ordinary investigators would miss."

"So why are you so interested in this stiff that the papers haven't learned the true identity of; someone you know?" I said flatly.

Philpot turned and looked out the large window before he spoke. After several seconds he said, "The murdered man was my brother. He'd changed his name so as not to disgrace the family and was going by the name Jim Conley. I guess he picked that name because that was his best friend's name. He was killed while serving in the Air Force in Rhein Main Germany, just out of Frankfurt. Anyway, that was when Eric, that's my brother's real name, looked for solace at the bottom of a glass or bottle."

He paused for a few seconds and then continued on.

"Eric and I were never real close. I was more serious and goal oriented. He was a happy-go-lucky kind of guy that looked at work as a necessity. He hated it, but held a steady job until the real Jim Conley's death. Within six months from Jim's death he'd lost his job and was living in a flop house on the corner of Walk and Don't Walk; I really don't know where he called home. I know one thing though, I can't let his murderer go free, even it was just another drunk that killed him," Philpot said as he turned back towards me. I thought I saw the glisten of a tear in his eye.

"So the question to you, Mr. Quinn, is this; will you take the case?"

I didn't jump at the opportunity right away, although I wanted to, but rather tried to determine in my own mind if I was up to the task. I hadn't done real investigative work since I'd been forced to retire and really didn't know if I could do the job anymore. Somehow a verse of Bible scripture from my days in Sunday school made its way out of the dark crevices of my brain and into the light of my current thoughts. The verse was simple yet power packed with truth, "As a man thinks, so is he." Don't ask me book, chapter, and verse. The thought was so overwhelming it made me gasp.

"I'll take the job, Mr. Philpot. Yes, I'll take it, and I'll find out who it was that killed your brother," I said with a confidence I had not felt for years.

Philpot started to smile, but didn't. Instead he sat down at his desk and opened a large check book and began to write. When he'd finished he tore a check out of the book and handed it across the desk in my direction.

"You've got two weeks to come up with something, Mr. Quinn. If you haven't found out anything of substantial importance in that time, we'll call it off. I'll be able to rest knowing that I at least made an attempt to find my brother's killer. Then I'll just figure it was a fight between a couple of drunks that cost my brother his life, and let it drop. This is a retainer for your services and I'll pay you a thousand dollars a day and you pay your expenses out of that. Do we have a deal?"

I looked at the amount of the check he'd handed me and it was for five thousand dollars. I hadn't seen that much money at one time since...well, let me just say, a very long time. I folded the check and stuck it in my inside coat pocket. I was just about to tell Philpot that I'd take the job when he spoke.

"I'll expect you to stay sober while you're investigating this; you do understand that, don't you? I'm not paying you for an extended drinking bout. I'll want you to check in with either me, or my secretary everyday. One day you don't check in and I'll figure you've tanked and are passed out somewhere and you're off the payroll. I hate to be so blunt, but that's the way it is," Philpot said, his eyebrows knitted firmly together.

He had every right to demand his money's worth. He was taking a chance that I wouldn't just take his five grand and head for the nearest bar and stay drunk till the money ran out. I had a feeling this was a chance for me to take control of my life again. As I started to answer Philpot that verse of scripture loomed again in my mind, causing me to blink hard as the words seemed to explode in my brain, "As a man thinks, so is he."

Philpot noticed that something was taking place with me and cocked his head to one side questioningly.

"Are you all right, Mr. Quinn?"

"Yes, yes; I just want to tell you that you don't have to worry. Not only will I stay sober, but I'll find your brother's killer," I stated meaning every word I said.

Philpot looked at me analytically for several seconds and then smiled that even, white teeth smile of his, "I think you really mean that, Mr. Quinn; I really do."

We shook hands and I left with a new lease on life. This was a chance for me to become a real person again; and not just someone that lived to drink a drink that was slowly killing me. The next forty eight hours would be rough, I knew that, but I was ready for it. I had five thousand dollars in my pocket with the promise of nine thousand more if I could stay sober for two weeks. But the real plum was waiting at the end of the two weeks. I would be free of Jack Daniels and could once again concentrate on what I was; a real detective.

CHAPTER

3

I **WALKED out of Rod Philpot's office feeling** wonderful about life, and something else; something I had not felt good about for years; myself. This gig for Philpot had been a godsend; that was for sure. I had been living a life of nothingness for so long it had begun to look like something. Now I could see the difference.

The whole world took on a different look and feel as I made my way across the busy street to where I'd parked my badly dented car. As I unlocked the door I compared the car's state of being to my own. The exterior of the car was badly banged up and the engine was in need of a tune-up. The paint was peeling off the top of the car as well as the hood and trunk. The tires were so thin you could almost see the air in them, but the interior looked pretty good when compared to the rest of the car.

That was a lot like me, I surmised. My body had been banged around, dented up, and busted in places. My clothes looked like they'd all came off a rack at Goodwill or the Salvation Army Store. I was so out of shape I couldn't even say the words 'Gold's Gym' without breaking into a sweat and huffing and puffing like I'd just run the Boston Marathon.

But there was something inside me that still held some value to someone; God; and now, me! That verse of scripture had been there all the time; ever since I'd first heard it. "As a man thinks, so is he." The words carried such depth and true, life changing power. As I continued to dwell on that phrase it seemed to come alive. If a man thinks about murder, he will eventually carry it out. If a man thinks about lying, he will become a liar. If he thinks about booze, he'll become a boozer. In other words, what you think yourself to be, you will become.

I knew there was a deeper object lesson here than just that, but right now what I'd come to understand was enough. I would definitely delve deeper into this verse at a later date.

My eight year old, going on twenty, Dodge started, but not before belching out a cloud of black smoke, totally consuming the car parked directly behind mine and completely obscuring it from my vision in my car's rearview mirror. I knew that would be a picture of me in a few days; belching out blackness from my own insides.

I headed straight for police headquarters with the hope that Chief Wells might have meant what he said to Philpot. If the police were not going to give this a thorough investigation they might be willing to toss me a few bones in way of what they knew about the case. It was worth a try, anyway.

I had made a couple of visits back to the police station I had called home, from time to time, but not recently. It's not easy facing people that you worked with after being let go like I had been; pride or embarrassment being the motivating factor there, I guess. Everyone wants to look like they're doing well, but when you look like I did now, the look betrays you.

That last bit of realization hit me hard. Here I am riding around with a check for five thousand dollars in my pocket and wearing a suit that I'd bought at Savers for fourteen bucks. Somehow the two realities didn't fit well together.

Upon seeing the bank that I do business with, well, in a manner of speaking that is; after all I did have a checking account with them that contained twenty four dollars and twelve cents; I pulled into the parking lot. I went inside and proudly filled out a deposit slip for the check, less five hundred dollars. A man of my means needs walking around money, you know.

After gorging my anemic account with the forty five hundred clams I headed for a new clothes clothing store; one that actually sold new clothes. I'd seen an ad in Sunday's paper that Sears was having a sale on suits and figured there was no better time than now to start changing my image. It would definitely help my pride if I could go into the stationhouse wearing a good looking suit.

Sears came through, big time. I got a good deal on a charcoal gray suit, a matching shirt and tie combination, along with a new pair of shoes and still had several hundred bucks in my wallet. I looked on the outside the way I was feeling on the inside; sharp.

I told the clerk I would wear the suit seeing as how the pants didn't need to be altered; the suit wasn't that expensive. I put my old suit in a shopping bag but deposited it in a trash receptacle that was just outside the store. Hey, I had a new suit now.

The car started again, drawing a few glares from the environmentalists passing by that didn't appreciate the black smoke fouling the air. I waved to them hoping they would notice the beautiful new suit I had on; from their reactions they either didn't notice or didn't care.

When I got to police headquarters I parked a block away, maybe feeling that my car didn't match with my new suit of clothes. It's kind of hard to appear well off when you get out of a car that looks like it was the winner in a destruction derby; or one of the last losers.

The first person I ran into was an old friend named Jeff Curtis. He had been my partner at the time I was promoted to homicide detective. He was a lieutenant now, also working homicide. Jeff looked up from his paperwork and cast a casual eye in my direction. He returned his gaze to his reading, but suddenly snapped his head up, doing a double take on me.

"Well, I'll be...Harley Quinn. How are you doing podna," he said, using a term we'd used for each other way back when.

"Hello Jeff; I see you've been busy climbing the ladder of success," I said in reference to his rank.

"You know what they say around here, Harley, "work or die." How've you been, Harley? I hear you've been a little down on your luck."

Jeff was never one to beat around a bush if he could go right through it. I liked that about him; he didn't waste any time. That's what made him a good cop.

"Do I look like I'm down on my luck," I said, making a slow pirouette so he could get an eyeful of my new duds.

Jeff grinned, "Hey, that suit belies what I heard. What are you doing for yourself now? Are you still working privately?"

"Yeah, I am Jeff. I'm working for Rodney Philpot. He hired me to see if I can turn up anything on the Jim Conley murder."

"Jim Conley? Oh, yeah, the derelict murder case. We've got one or two leads, but nothing you can count on as leading anywhere. Have you ever tried to question a bunch of drunks about another drunk?" Jeff suddenly caught his own words and his eyes widened slightly. "Uh, no offense, Harley; I didn't mean it that way."

"Hey, no offense taken; besides that was the case at one time; but no more," I said, shocked at my own statement and its sincerity.

21

Jeff smiled approvingly, "Good, podna, good."

"What I was wondering Jeff, was this; do you have anything you might be able to share with me?" I asked.

Jeff was just about to answer when Captain Jaime Bruce of the homicide division walked by. He looked at Jeff and started to say something, but stopped when he recognized me.

"Harley...what brings you down here; business I hope," he said as he extended his hand for a friendly handshake.

"Hello Captain. How're you doing?" I said to my old captain.

"Fine, thanks, and I'd say you are too. Great looking suit you have on there," Jaime said standing back and taking a good look at me.

"What, this old thing," I said modestly.

"It isn't too old, Harley; you forgot to remove this tag off the sleeve here," he said pointing to the tag tacked near the end of the sleeve.

"Whoops, I guess I missed that one," I said, my embarrassment obviously showing.

"Hey, don't worry about it. If it wasn't for my wife people would know my size and the cost of everything I wear," Jaime said shrugging it off.

"I'd better get me a wife then," I laughed.

Jaime and Jeff laughed also and then Jaime took on a more businesslike look.

"What does bring you down here, Harley?"

"Actually, Captain, I was telling Jeff here, that I'm working for Rodney Philpot. He wants me to see what I can turn up on the Conley murder case; he's the derelict that was found with his throat cut a few weeks back. I guess the Chief told Philpot that you won't be spending too much time on this case. I hoped you might be willing to share some information with me...for old time's sake, so to speak."

Jaime grinned, "It would be my pleasure. It's good to see you working again, Harley; it really is," the Captain said and then looked at Lt. Curtis. "Jeff, you give him what we have on the case and any other info that might be helpful to him."

"Sure thing, Captain; I'll take care of him," Jeff said with a quick grin.

"Take care, Harley; don't be a stranger," the Captain said and moved on towards his office.

"He's a great guy, Jeff; treat him good," I said watching Jaime walk away.

"He's the best. Well, Harley, let me bring you up to date on this murder case," Jeff said and pulled up a file from his desk drawer.

Jeff went over the evidence the police had on the murder case with me, which wasn't much. The body of the victim, Jim Conley, a.k.a. Eric Philpot, had been found by a garbage truck driver in a large dumpster in the shadiest part of town. His throat had been cut from ear to ear and with such force that the victims head was almost completely severed. There were no witnesses and no one had much to say; not to the cops anyway.

The police figured the killer to be a big man and strong considering the amount of strength it would take to inflict such a wound. The coroner also determined by the angle of the cut that the victim was either sitting or squatting down when killed. If he was standing, the murderer would have to be somewhere close to seven feet tall. One thing was for sure; if the killer was that tall he'd be well known around that area of town. Otherwise, he'd have to be a visitor there.

I took what little information the police had to go on and headed for the rescue mission that the police said

23

was only about two blocks from where the murder had occurred. Contrary to popular belief, I had not reached that low a place in life that I hung out in the bars down this low in the chain of society; not yet I hadn't.

As I drove I thought of the people I'd be questioning and the area of town I'd be asking those questions in. Suddenly I realized that I still had not removed the tag off my new suit and that's when it hit me. I needed that old suit of mine. I couldn't get the kind of openness I'd need wearing a brand new suit and having cop written all over me.

I made a detour and went back by the Sears store where I'd dumped my old suit in the trash can. Finding a parking space right in front of it was more than I could ask, but I did. Fortunately the trash had not been picked up yet and after removing a couple of half filled containers of Starbuck's Coffee; I knew people didn't really like that stuff; retrieved my now coffee stained suit.

The coffee stains would fit right in with the territory now. I just hoped I didn't run into anyone I knew while wearing this monstrosity. A few people cast curious stares at someone wearing a suit like the one I had on, going through a trash receptacle. They really did a double take when they saw me pull the old suit out of the bin and toss it in the front seat of my car.

A nearby gas station's restroom provided me with a changing area. I put my new suit, shirt, matching tie, and shoes in the trunk of the car. I didn't want to take a chance on someone seeing them, not where I was going. They wouldn't let a locked car stop them from laying their hands on something like a new suit. I also found an old dress hat that I had tossed in the trunk a few months back and forgotten about. I took it out and stuck it on my head, an added touch to my look as a regular in the lower part of town.

When I reached the rescue mission I parked about a block and a half away and made the walk back to where it was located. I passed a couple of old timers that didn't hit me up for any money so I figured I must look as down on my luck as they were.

It was between meals so there weren't very many people hanging around the mission. I walked in and gave the place the once over. There were six rows of bench type pews split down the middle and on each side. The walls were a light tan color with water stains in spots, hopefully from the rain. The floors were concrete with worn rugs in the aisles and across the front near the pulpit. Off to the right side there was a door that, I presumed, led to the kitchen. I headed in that direction.

I could hear voices coming from behind the door as I neared it. One of the voices was distinctly that of a woman. The others were men's voices; two, I figured. They were talking and laughing as though they knew one another quite well.

I pushed the door open carefully and looked in. It was the kitchen and there were two men and a woman busy preparing the evening meal. The woman was peeling potatoes, cutting them in half and tossing them into a huge pot of water. The men were shucking corn that someone had obviously donated to them. When they saw me they all three stopped speaking and waited for me to say something.

"Hi, I'm looking for the head rescuer," I said, attempting to make a joke.

It went over like a lead balloon. When I saw that they weren't interested in my jokes, I tried the truth.

"My name is Harley Quinn and I'm looking for the pastor of the mission," I said a little more humbly this time.

"I'm Rev. Erin Richard, can I help you?"

"I hope so, Reverend. I'm investigating the murder that occurred about two blocks from here a short while back and I was wondering if you knew anything about it," I asked seriously.

The Reverend looked at me with a curious eye. I knew what he was thinking so I attempted to put his mind at ease.

"I thought I'd fit in with the locals if I dressed the part. You know what they say about people hearing what they see. I figured I'd make them see what they expected and then maybe they'll hear what I have to say.

The reverend grinned, "I like that...people hear what they see. Do you mind if I use that in one of my sermons sometime?"

"Be my guest," I smiled. "I got it from a movie I saw. It does carry a lot of truth in it, however. I'm not going to listen to something on aerodynamics from a guy wearing bib overall's and holding a pitchfork. If the people down here think they're talking to one of their own, they may say things they wouldn't otherwise."

The man standing next to the pastor interjected at that point, "You asked if the pastor knew anything about the murder down here; uh, I heard some scuttlebutt about that killing."

"Oh, what did you hear?"

"Two of the people close to Jim; that was the victim's name, Jim Conley, said that they saw him in the company of a very tall man. Jim was around six one or two and this man towered over him. They said the two of them were in front of a liquor store down the street. The man gave Jim some money and waited outside while Jim went in and bought a bottle. They said they'd never seen the man before or since then. Jim's body was found the next morning in an alleyway about three blocks from there," the man said.

"Hmm, that goes right along with the coroner's report. The report said that the victim would either have to have been sitting, or kneeling, otherwise the killer would have to stand around seven feet tall. It sounds like the latter could be the truth. But they said they didn't think he was from around here, huh?" I pressed.

"No, the people I was talking to had never seen him before. There's one person you might talk to, however, that seems to know everyone that is a regular down here. Her name is Darlene Hawkins, but everyone around here knows her as Duchess. You can usually find her across from the Rite Aid store just down the street. Give her a kind word and she'll talk your leg off," the man said.

"Thank you..."

"Gus...Gus Hazifotis, I'm the assistant pastor here. This pretty lady over here is Jeri Munoz. She's the best cook in the state of Washington," Gus grinned.

"Oh, go on, Gus. He knows we're having cherry pie for dessert tonight and he's looking for double helping, that's all," Jeri smiled.

They all three seemed so happy, so content, I thought to myself. There was a peace about them that money certainly can't buy. I liked them right away.

Pastor Richard suddenly took on a more serious expression, "You know...now that I think about it, I do remember seeing a very tall man walking down the street very late on the night the murder was to have occurred. I remember it now because of what you said earlier about, you hear what you see.

"I had stayed late after we'd closed up for the night to do some paper work and finished up around eight o'clock. I had a cup of coffee and then I locked up and headed for home. I had just turned the corner at the end of the block when a very tall man started off the curb but pulled back when he saw my car. I had the radio set on an oldies station and just as I saw this tall man, the song 'Big, Bad John' started playing. I remember smiling at the coincidence. Maybe it wasn't a coincidence after all," the pastor said with a slight frown.

"That's interesting, Pastor, because the coroner estimated the killing to have taken place sometime between nine and nine thirty. That very well could have been the killer; if the killer is a tall man, that is. Did you tell the police any of this?"

"No I didn't say anything to the police at that time, because they didn't mention anything about a tall man possibly being a suspect. I'm not sure I would have recalled it at that time even if they had asked," the pastor explained.

Gus chimed in then, "I didn't hear that about the tall man being in Jim's company until two days ago, myself. I meant to call the police, but to be honest with you, I simply forgot. That might sound a little callous, but it's true."

"I doubt that it would have gone very far in their pursuit of the guilty party, anyway," I said. "They've put this one on a back burner and it will eventually go out altogether. But since I'm working for a private individual I'll definitely be following up on the leads you've given me. Could you give me a list of names of people that were close to Conley; I'd like to talk to them."

'Sure thing, but the list won't be very long. Jim was a sullen man that didn't let too many people get near him. I'd say the two that I was talking to were about the only ones he'd even let get close to him. Well, not counting the Duchess, that is. Everyone loves her."

"Any names are more than I have now."

"Sure let me write them down for you. I'll also write the area they hang out in the most; other than here," Gus smiled.

"There was another killing down here about four weeks ago. The man was stabbed in the stomach and left to die in an alleyway also. He managed to crawl to the street where he was spotted by a passing motorist who called 911. Did you happen to read about that?" Pastor Erin asked.

"No, I don't remember reading that," I said.

I didn't bother telling him there were a lot of things I didn't remember due to the fact that I was lost in a bottle for days at a time and hadn't read anything but the bottle label.

"The police checked on it, but they didn't come around very often. I don't know if they found any leads on that case or not. I know I haven't read anymore about it in the paper," Pastor Erin went on.

"What was that victim's name, do you recall?"

"Oh, yeah; he was a regular here at the mission. All we knew him by around here was Blinky. He had an eye condition that caused him to blink almost uncontrollably. Some days it was worse than others, though. No one that I know of ever knew his given name."

"If anyone did know it, though; it would be the Duchess. She's a walking information booth when it comes to folks down here," Gus said as he finished writing out the list for me.

"I'll check it out and see if there's a connection to Conley's murder," I said taking the paper from Pastor Hazifotis. "I guess now I should go and talk to the Duchess, Darlene Hawkins."

I thanked them for their cooperation and asked them to keep it under their hats about a private investigator working undercover down here. They assured me they would and I left. I found the Duchess with no trouble. The trouble was when I found her she was dead.

CHAPTER

4

THERE WAS a rather large crowd gathered outside the Rite Aid building when I arrived there. I made my way through the crowd and saw a lady that appeared to be in her late sixties lying on the ground. No one had to tell me who she was; I knew instantly.

"What happened," I asked as I knelt down beside the woman and looked around at the serious faces staring down at her.

"I saw the whole thing. She was just standing there on the corner selling her pencils when out of nowhere a pickup truck came barreling down the street and ran up over the curb, hitting her and knocking her into the side of the building right there," a man said as he pointed towards the spot where the Duchess had hit the wall.

"Then the pickup took off down the street that way," he said pointing towards the cross street. "I know the guy must have been drunk or crazy. He didn't even attempt to see if he could help her or not. I'll bet he ruined a wheel when he hit the curb like he did. This poor woman never stood a chance," he continued excitedly.

"Did you get a look at the driver?" I asked.

"Not really, but I can describe the vehicle to a tee."

"First things first; do you think the driver may have been a tall man?" I asked hopefully.

"Now how would I know that? The man was in his pickup," the witness snapped.

"Think about it; was he hunched over the steering wheel, or was his head even with it," I pushed.

"Now that you mention it, he must have been a tall man, in fact, a very tall man. He was hunched way over the steering wheel of the pickup. I remember thinking that he looked too big for the size of the vehicle he was driving. It was one of the small pickups, you know," the man said with a studious look on his face.

"Okay, now what kind of a pickup was it," I asked hopefully.

The man grinned proudly, "A Ford Ranger, the small model. It was white and didn't have a license plate yet. It just had that new paper one in the back window."

"Did you get the number?"

"No, I'm sorry, I didn't. But I did notice something else about the pickup," the man said and then waited for me to coax the answer out of him.

"Well, what was it," I said after several long seconds of silence.

"It had a Seattle Seahawks sticker on the bumper. That's why I noticed the pickup didn't have a rear license plate. But like I said, it did have a Seattle Seahawks bumper sticker," the man said proudly.

"Was it last years model or this year's," I asked knowing that some car lots give great deals on new cars that they still had on hand from the year before when they get the new models in.

The man cocked his head as if I had asked him a trick question, "Well if it was new it would have to be this year's model, wouldn't it? Oh, I see what you mean. I don't know if it was last year's model or this year to be perfectly frank with you. I can't see much of a change in cars from one year to the next. I personally don't know why they make a new car every single year. They'd sell more if they only came out with new ones every other year, I think."

There must be five to six hundred Ford Rangers driving around Seattle with Seahawks bumper stickers on them. New ones, however, narrowed the field considerably. I told the man to stick around until the police got there and he said he would. I'd no sooner made that statement than a patrol car pulled up shortly before the paramedics.

I slipped into the crowd and disappeared. After all I couldn't give the police any information on the hit and run, or about the victim, for that matter. The fact that the man said the driver must have been a tall man made me wonder if it could possibly be the same man that had been seen with Eric Philpot, better known around here as Jim Conley.

On the way to my car I spotted several pencils lying on the ground, obviously ones that the Duchess had been offering for sale. I picked one up, not to use but to keep as a remembrance. I wished she was alive so I could pay her.

The other man that had been killed named Blinky kept coming to mind. He, too, had been knifed, but not in the same way as Rodney Philpot's brother. I had a sneaky suspicion that the two cases had something in common, but what?

I had almost reached my car when another thought hit me.

"Cassandra," I said out loud.

I'd promised her I'd call her and let her know the outcome of the meeting I'd had with Philpot and it had completely slipped my mind. Actually that was a good sign. When I'd been on the force, before Jack had taken control of me, I had a tendency to get so involved in murder cases that I'd forget trivial things; things like paying phone bills, electric bills, meeting dental appointments. The case I'd be working on consumed my every waking thought. That was a good thing and a bad thing all at once. Work wise it was great, socially and responsibly it wasn't so great.

I found a pay phone and fortunately had enough change to call Cass. She was ecstatic about my getting the job and the fact that I'd bought a new suit and shoes. She was responsible for what few good clothes I had in my closet. I usually saved them for my dates with her.

The one thing I didn't mention to Cass was my new found desire to kick the booze. I didn't want to sound like so many other drunks that are always saying they're going on the wagon, only to fall off it three days later. Actions speak louder than words do anyway.

I told her I'd tell her more about my day when I saw her later that evening. She told me to come to her apartment around six thirty and she'd have dinner ready. I promised I'd be there on time, something I wasn't in the habit of doing. Cass didn't sound too convinced. On dinner dates where she was doing the cooking she always prepared something that would taste good the second day in case I failed to show up when planned. As an added surprise I told her I'd bring the wine. She said fine, but I could hear the disappointment in her voice.

I decided to walk back to the area around the rescue mission and leave my car where it was parked. Somehow I'd managed to find a broken parking meter that was stuck on five minutes. You have to take advantage of things like that.

I saw a liquor store down the street and knew that I would have to have something to offer the guys that were on the list that Gus had given me. If you want a drunk to talk offer him something to drink. Anything with alcohol in it would do, but it couldn't be too expensive or they'd know I wasn't on the level. A bottle of Muscatel or Tokay would be to their liking and not raise suspicions.

Entering the liquor store would be my first real test at dumping Daniels. I looked around the store at all the different brands of wine, whiskey, beer, and even cordials. Suddenly I felt my hands begin to sweat and that flushed, warm sensation that always seemed to consume my body in an invisible flame when I wanted a drink; the one that started with my face and neck and worked its way down to the soles of my feet. I caught myself licking my lips nervously.

The weakness in my knees made me close my eyes. I could feel JD's pull on me; drawing me towards him. I swallowed hard as I moved in the direction of the whiskey. Standing before the rack laden with bottles of Jack Daniels, Jim Beam, Wild Turkey, and Canadian Club I felt weak all over.

My hand trembled slightly as I started to reach for the bottle of Jack Daniels. My fingers couldn't have been more than an inch away from the bottle when the words flashed brilliantly in my mind's eye; "As a man thinks, so is he."

The thought was so overwhelming it caused me to pull my hand back like it had grabbed a hot electrical wire. My eyes widened as the thought took hold. I was thinking and reacting to those thoughts, like a drunk. Thoughts are the controlling factor in our actions and I wasn't about to let these thoughts control me anymore.

"I'm a private investigator," I said out loud; loud enough that the customer nearest me answered.

"Oh, is that right? Well I'm a Supreme Court Justice," he said with a slight slur, causing me to look in his direction.

He was a man desperately in need of a bath, a shave, new clothes, and a hot meal. I looked at him and felt sorry for both of us; but especially him. As I looked at him I suddenly saw me in five years if I didn't quit drinking. It literally made me gasp.

The man grabbed a bottle of something, I didn't really notice what, and weaved towards the cash register. I turned quickly away from the whiskey rack and walked to the wine section of the store. I hurriedly grabbed a bottle of Thunderbird off the shelf and walked up front to pay for it.

The further I got from the whiskey bottles the less pull they had on me. I couldn't help but think of another quote from the Bible; "Resist the devil and he will flee from you." That could also be, "Resist temptation and it will flee from you." It was amazing how the further away from the store I got, the less the need for a drink. But I wasn't fooling myself; I knew that the worst was yet to come.

CHAPTER

5

THE FIRST NAME on the list was Harry
Hahn. There was a notation next to his name that
simply read, Rico's. I'd heard of Rico Calderon,
the owner of the place. He'd been hauled in a few times
when I was on the force for passing funny money. We
could never prove that he hadn't received it from one of
his customers, which is what he always claimed, so we
had never been able to drop the hammer on him.

I doubted that Rico would be able to place me since I
was never one of the cops that rousted him. I just knew
who he was by seeing him at the precinct and from what
the other cops had told me about him. His place was as
dirty as he was; maybe more so.

As I walked towards the long bar that ran the entire
length of one wall in the seriously darkened bar, I could
hear, as well as feel, the soles of my shoes being tugged at
by the slight adhesiveness of something that had been
spilled on the floor and allowed to dry there. I just hoped
it was booze of some kind. The place had an odor of
cheap wine and cheaper perfume. The perfume odor
came from the three women that were seated in various
parts of the barroom.

I sat down on a stool, but not before feeling it to
make sure it hadn't been coated with the same sticky
substance that was on the floor. I'd no sooner sat down

than one of the three women in the joint made a move on me. They didn't waste time or words in this part of town.

"Say Big Boy, buy a lady a drink?" the woman said.

Since there were no women on the list that Gus had given me, I felt safe in telling the woman to beat it.

"Drift," I said without looking at the woman who was obviously the major source of the cheap perfume's aroma.

"What," she asked in a surprised voice.

"Beat it; I ain't got the money for you and me both," I lied.

"Well, thanks for nothing. I hope you get Aids and die," she said as she made her way back down to the end of the bar.

"The bartender walked slowly down the length of the bar and stopped in front of me.

"Give me a...beer," I said, not saying the first thing that had come to my mind.

"Bottle or draft," the bartender asked.

"Draft if it's cheaper," I said knowing it would be. I had to look and sound down on my luck.

"Coming up," he said and walked away.

I fished out a five dollar bill and made sure the bag with the bottle of Thunderbird was securely tucked away in my pocket. I laid the five on the bar and looked at the other patrons in the bar.

The bar had a total of nine people in it. There were four men patrons in the bar, two at the bar and two with the other two women in the joint; the woman that hit me up for a drink, the bartender, and me. I wondered if one of the four men could possibly be Harry Hahn.

When the bartender returned with my beer I asked him, "Hey, has Harry been in today?"

The bartender looked at me curiously, "Harry who?"

"Hahn, Harry Hahn; I have something for him; has he been in or not?"

The bartender looked at me without blinking an eye but didn't say anything for a few seconds.

After lighting a cigarette and blowing a puff of bluish colored smoke in the air, due to the rooms lighting, he spoke up, "No, but he should be in before long. It's nearing cocktail hour."

I looked at the fluorescent clock on the wall behind the bar and saw that it was nearing five o'clock. I would have to leave in another forty five minutes if I was to be at Cassandra's on time, and I didn't want to be late getting to her place. I hoped Harry would hurry up and get here.

"Do you know what Harry looks like," the bartender questioned.

I started to say yes, but something told me to be up front. After all, Harry could be one of the guys in the bar right now. I went with my gut feeling.

"No, actually I don't. I know, or I should say, knew, a friend of Harry's; Jim Conley. I have something of Jim's I know he'd want Harry to have. Will you let me know when he comes in?"

The bartender smiled knowingly, "Sure. In fact, he's here already. That's him in the end booth down there, the one with the babe."

I looked in the direction he nodded and saw the back of a man's head. Sitting across from the man, and facing me, was a bleached blond. It was so bleached I could tell it even in the darkness of the bar; which by now, my eyes were becoming accustomed to.

"What's the babe's name," I asked.

"Dolly; you'll know why when you get a good look at her," the bartender grinned, his cigarette dangling from one corner of his mouth. By using his tongue only he shifted the cigarette to the other corner of his mouth. "She used to work the Frolic Room in Frisco. That's where I first knew her from. She was the best stripper on the West Coast in those days. What a woman," he said gazing longingly towards the woman.

"Is she Harry's steady," I questioned.

"Steady? No, Dolly doesn't go in for steadies; she likes a variety. To quote her, 'variety is the spice of life.' No, one man ain't enough for Dolly. You'll see, just wait till you meet her."

I waited until the bartender had brought my change to me and then picked up my beer and walked to the back booth. The woman, Dolly, looked up as I approached and said something to Harry. Harry turned around and looked in my direction and moved to the edge of the booth seat. I didn't want to take any chances on spooking him, so I spoke before I got too close to them.

"Say, Harry, I have something I want to give to you that be...," that's as far as I got before Harry sprang from the booth and ran passed me, giving me a hard shove that sent me flying into the empty booth behind theirs.

Harry moved more like a track star than a drunk on skid row. He was out the front door and halfway to Tacoma before I extracted myself out of the empty booth. Dolly didn't offer to help me to my feet, but spoke once I was upright again.

"Thanks a lot. You just ran my dinner date off and I'm starving," Dolly said with her agitation clearly expressed in her tone.

"Oh, sorry about that; what's with that guy, anyway," I asked?

"Everybody's jumpy down here, Mister; didn't you know that? There's someone knocking off the regulars to this part of town and it's scary. At least the guys are scared. So far they're the only ones getting bumped off," Dolly said easily, her irritation slowly fading as she talked.

"Is that right? You mean Jim Conley and Blinky," I said quickly so she'd figure me to be from around here.

"Yeah, you know Jim and Blinky?"

"Just casually, not really what you'd call friends. I knew Jim a little better than I did Blinky, though. Did you know that Jim's real name was Eric Philpot?" I said hoping to score enough points with Dolly that she'd introduce me around.

"You're kidding? Eric Philpot...you knew him better than I did. Who'd you get that from, the Duchess?"

"The Duchess; no, not the Duchess," I paused. "I guess you haven't heard yet, huh?"

"Heard what," Dolly asked seriously.

"I'm sorry to say that the Duchess was killed a little while ago; a hit and run," I said sadly.

Dolly looked shocked as her mouth dropped open slightly, "The Duchess, dead? A hit and run, you say?"

I nodded slowly, "Yeah, it happened down on her corner in front of the Rite Aid Store. Who'd want to kill such a sweet old gal as Duchess," I said.

"No one from around here, I can tell you that. If she was killed it had to be an accident. Everybody loved the Duchess. Why, she was like a saint around here. Always had a good word for you; a smile; a pat on the back. She was aces. Did you see it?" Dolly asked soulfully.

"No, I got there just after it happened. The police hadn't even arrived yet. One of the eyewitnesses said the driver was a very tall man driving a white Ford Ranger pickup; a new one. Do you know anyone like that around here?" I said, hoping to draw something out of Dolly. I did.

"Did you say a very tall man?" Dolly asked with fear in her eyes.

"Yeah, a very tall man, why?"

Dolly shook her head negatively, "That's what has all the men so jumpy down here. Blinky was seen with a very tall man not long before his body was found, and so was Jim. The boys think the tall man is the one that killed them. Now you say a very tall man killed the Duchess; maybe he's going after women now."

"Maybe the Duchess knew something she shouldn't have known. Did she ever say anything to you that would make you think she knew anything about a tall man around here?" I pressed, but not too hard.

"The Duchess said she didn't think the tall man was from around here at all. She said she saw a man that was very tall driving passed her corner on several occasions. He was definitely from the better part of town. She said she saw the same man, but driving two different cars. One time he got out and went inside Rite Aid, and that's when she saw how tall he really was; but she really didn't know if he was the one that was seen with Blinky and Jim shortly before they were murdered, because she never saw them with anyone. It was Harry and DuBonnet, the Frenchman. They're the ones that saw Jim with the tall man."

DuBonnet was the other name on the list that Gus had given me, along with the nickname, 'The Frenchman.'

"What about Blinky; who saw him in the company of a taller man? I asked, knowing now that the two cases were joined together like Siamese twins.

"That would be...Wallace. He said he saw Blinky with a very tall man a couple hours before Blinky crawled out of the alley and died before the paramedics could get there. Wallace got a good look at the man from what I hear. But Wallace is a hard man to find. He doesn't come around an awful lot. You'll just have to be around here when he shows up, 'cause I don't know where he calls home," Dolly said.

She'd really been helpful whether she knew it or not. I'd have to tell her to relay the message on to Harry and the Frenchman that I'd like to talk to them about the deaths of Conley and Blinky.

"Are you going to drink that beer, or just carry it around," Dolly asked, motioning towards the glass of draught beer I'd been holding, but not drinking.

I grinned, "No, actually I was bringing it to Harry. If you want it, you've got it." I said and slid the glass across the table to her.

"Well, listen Dolly; I'd really like to talk to Harry about Jim and Blinky, would you pass that along to him and the Frenchman for me?"

"Yeah, I will. Thanks for the beer, big spender," Dolly said with a sly grin.

"Thank you, Dolly. Oh, here's a card where you can reach me," I said handing her one of the few business cards I had.

She looked at it approvingly at first, but then frowning, "Harley Quinn, Private Investigator. I don't think you'll get a lot of cooperation from the folks around here. They clam up when cops come around; public or private."

"That card is for you, not for them. As far as they know the phone number belongs to a janitor, or a night watchman, or a taxi driver. They don't have to know about my line of work. Besides, I'm out to nail the one that's killing them off. Impress that upon them and I know that once they think about it, they'll come around," I said confidently.

"I'll do it for you, Harley; but only for what's in the bag?"

I pulled the paper bag containing the bottle of Thunderbird out of my pocket and handed it over to her. She checked the cap to make sure it hadn't been tampered with; once satisfied the bottle was full and the screw off cap was still sealed tight, she stated.

"I'll get them to talk to you, Harley. You just leave it up to me. I'm trusting that you're a straight shooter and not down here to bust any of my boys," Dolly said trying to come across with that little girl pout, but only managing to look childish.

It was time I headed for Cassandra's place. I had to stop and pick up a bottle of wine. I went back to the liquor store where I'd bought the Thunderbird, and picked up the wine we'd be having with dinner that evening. As I climbed into my car I lay the bottle of wine on the passenger's seat. I couldn't wait to see the look on Cass's face when she went to pour the Martinelli's Sparkling Cider. One thing was for sure; she'd be very pleased with my selection; and you could bet your life on that.

CHAPTER
6

CASSANDRA **looked stunned when she saw** me standing at her door in my new duds that I'd changed back into after leaving Rico's Bar.

"Harley; is that really you," she said and then looking at her watch added, "and on time?"

"And with the wine," I said as I handed her the paper bag with the Martinelli's Sparkling Cider, which she didn't look at right away.

"I love that suit...with matching shirt and tie, no less; and the shoes, too, none the less. My, oh my, aren't we looking sharp," Cass said as she stepped back to admire my new look.

"This is just something I picked up off the rack, nothing fancy," I said feigning humility.

The aroma of the roast that Cassandra had cooked drifted out of the kitchen and beckoningly down the hall, finding a home in my nostrils and causing my mouth to water involuntarily.

"Hmm, hmm, something smells good besides you, baby," I said sniffing the air.

Cass laughed as she put her arms around my waist and looked up at me waiting for her greeting kiss; which I willingly planted on her full and yielding lips.

"Hmm, maybe this is better than the roast beef," I said as I pulled back and looked down into her beautiful face.

"Are you hungry?"

"You said it, baby," I leered.

"I mean for a good meal! I know how much you like roast beef, so I've been slaving away for hours cooking it...actually I put it in the crock pot when I left for work this morning and turned it off when I got home," Cass grinned.

"Sounds like a crock to me," I wisecracked.

"So, what kind of wine did you bring for dinner," Cass said as she removed her arms from around my waist and looked inside the bag. She slowly pulled the bottle out and read the label. She didn't look up at me for several seconds, but when she did there was a tear in the corner of each of her beautiful eyes along with a question.

"Harley...does this mean what I think it means?" Cass asked carefully.

I looked her straight in the eye when I answered, "It does; but, I'm taking it one day at a time. No great, grandiose promises, just one day at a time; okay?"

Cass smiled warmly, "That's a great way to start."

THE DINNER WAS EXCELLENT. You couldn't buy a meal anywhere in Seattle any more succulent than the one Cass had prepared. The roast beef was so tender you could cut it with your fork. The mashed potatoes were buttery and creamy smooth and could have been eaten without the delicious beef gravy. Toss in the tossed green salad and green beans, and add the hot dinner rolls and you've got a meal fit for a king, or better still, a private investigator.

I don't know if it was because of not being full of booze that made me so hungry or not; but whatever it was, I ate like a lumberjack after a hard day of 'felling' trees.

When we finished dinner I pushed back from the table and looked at my lovely hostess. I sighed deeply which made Cass laugh as she picked up my empty plate, that I'd refilled twice and, together with hers, set them on the drain board next to the sink. The best compliment you can pay a great cook is not by mere words, but by eating the meal as if you truly enjoy it; which I most assuredly had.

"Save room for some cheesecake," Cass said with a quick, double rising of her eyebrows.

"Cheesecake, are you going to model something for me?" I joked.

"Maybe after dessert," Cass shot back with a smile.

"You really do have cheesecake?" I said more seriously this time. Cass knew how much I loved cheesecake, especially the edible kind.

"Just for you, my dear; now, you go in and watch TV and enjoy your coffee, while I clean off the table," Cass said as she got up and poured me a cup of hot coffee.

"Let me help," I said, trying to sound sincere.

Cass shook her head, "No, you've pleased me enough with what you've already done. It won't take me a minute. Besides, I have a complete set of dishes and I want to keep them that way."

I took my coffee and went into the living room, flipping the TV on as I passed by it. It was Monday Night and the Seahawks were playing at home. The game was already in the second quarter and the Seahawks were ahead of Denver by the score of 10-7.

I had gotten out of the habit of watching football and it felt good to have a full stomach and relaxing in front of the tube and watching a game again. Cass liked football and especially when the Hawks, as they're called around here, were playing. I was actually surprised she hadn't had the game on when I arrived. That in itself was enough to tell me that something had occupied her mind; like my landing this gig with Philpot for instance.

Cass joined me shortly and snuggled up next to me on the sofa, curling her bare feet up under her as she nestled her head against my chest.

"I'd forgotten the Hawks were playing tonight. I was so absorbed in thinking about you getting the assignment with Rodney Philpot that it just slipped my mind. I'm so proud of you Harley. What's the score?"

"The Hawks are up by three, ten to seven."

I'd no sooner gotten the words out of my mouth when one of the Denver running backs broke through the line and galloped passed the linebackers into the open field. After a couple of "zigs" and "zags " he loped into the end zone where he instantly went into some kind of weird looking celebration.

It never ceases to amaze me how these guys carry on when they do something they're getting paid to do, score touchdowns, or make tackles, or catch passes. You don't see the offensive line celebrating after every play that keeps the defense out of the back field. Congratulations from their teammates should be enough.

Just as all this was running through my mind the camera cut to the Seattle sidelines and locked onto the faces of the various coaches. The head coach was furious, as was the defensive line coach, the linebackers coach, and the defensive backs coach. You could see the anger written across their faces as the veins bulged in their beefy necks and tight foreheads.

As the camera started to cut away I caught just a glimpse of someone in back of the players punching the huge container of Gatorade and almost knocking it over. The man had to have delivered a mighty blow to move the container as much as he had with his punch. I called it to Cass's attention but she'd missed it.

Naturally when the camera shot to the other side of the field there was jubilation. The coach there was hugging players coming off the field and patting them on the backs. His smile was so bright they could have turned the stadium lights off and still kept it well lit due to his grin.

"Oh, crap," Cass said from her comfortable position against me, not bothering to move.

"Hey, it's early in the game. The Hawks will come back," I said easily.

We watched the game until half time and by then I was ready for that cheesecake Cass had offered me. We sat at the kitchen table and ate; she telling me about her day and me telling her more about Rodney Philpot and my hopes of getting some high rolling clients because of him.

By the time we'd finished our dessert the game had started again. We went back to our previous positions on the sofa and watched the remainder of the game. It turned out to be a heartbreaker for the Hawks and their fans.

With just under a minute to go and the Hawks ahead by three points, the Hawks were forced to punt the ball away. The punt sailed off the side of the punter's foot and out of bounds for a net punt of twelve yards. Denver got the ball on their own forty-two yard line with just enough time to run three plays which went nowhere. On fourth down they put up a 'Hail Mary' pass into the end zone. I don't have to tell you what happened; but I will.

The ball sailed high into the air and came down into a crowd of receivers, most of them being Seahawk players. It hit the outstretched hands and bounced into the air again. When it came down it went through the hands of the scrambling players and towards the ground, where it landed in the chest of one of the Denver receiver's who'd been knocked down flat on his back. Touch down, game over!

There was a stunned silence in the stadium and you could hear it loud and clear over the TV. The camera panned the audience and mouths were agape all over the place. A few people were jumping up and down, obviously Denver fans, but the vast majority of people stood motionless, in a state of shock.

The camera once again went to the sidelines where there was stunned silence on one side of the field and pandemonium on the other side. Cass had moved to an upright position by this time and when I looked at her saw the same reaction as those on the screen.

Cass looked at me blankly, "I don't believe it."

"Neither do I," I answered.

"Want some more cheesecake," Cass said causing me to do a double take at her lack of emotion.

"What?"

"Hey, it's only a game, Harley. I'm too happy to let the outcome of a game rob me of this day and night," Cass smiled.

I couldn't help but think the same thing the bartender at Rico's Bar had said about Dolly, "What a woman."

EARLY THE NEXT MORNING I called Rodney Philpot's office and when I didn't get anyone but the answering machine left a brief message on it giving him a brief rundown on what I'd learned on my first day on the job.

I headed back down to the shady part of town and parked near the rescue mission. I had several people I wanted to talk to and they would be arriving for their breakfast, hopefully, around that time. I hoped that Dolly had given Harry Hahn the message that I only wanted to talk to him. I just hoped she didn't tell everyone about me being a private cop. My hopes were about to come to fruition or be dashed very shortly. Harry was walking down the street towards the mission in the company of Dolly and another man.

I got out of my car and stood by it so they couldn't miss seeing me. Dolly saw me first and waved, before saying something to the two men with her. When she did they both looked my way, but neither bolted. That was definitely a good sign.

As they neared me I moved towards them with a slight smile. Harry looked at me with a wary eye, but the other man showed no nervousness whatsoever. I held out my hand to Dolly who took it and slightly nodded her head.

"I told them that you were a friend of Jim Conley's and you'd just hit town," Dolly said, giving me a slight wink unnoticed by the two men.

"Thanks, Dolly. You're Harry Hahn, right?" I said turning my attention towards Hahn.

"Yeah, that's right. Sorry about yesterday, but we're all a little jumpy down here," Hahn said, still giving me the once over.

"Hi, my name is DuBonnet, but most people just call me the Frenchman," DuBonnet said extending his hand which looked fairly clean.

"Hello, my name is Harley Quinn. Jim Conley and I were friends, well somewhat; I know his brother a lot better than I knew Jim. He wanted me to see if I could find out who might have killed Jim. From what I hear you two saw him with a very tall man, is that right?"

DuBonnet took control of the other end of the conversation which suited me just fine. I like someone that talks a lot, especially when I'm asking the questions. DuBonnet was open and didn't hold back anything.

"Yes, we saw Jim and a very tall man at White's Liquor Store just down the street. The man gave Jim some money and Jim went inside the store while the man waited outside next to the building."

"Did you get a look at the tall man's face?" I asked hopefully.

"No...we didn't. He kept his face more towards the building, almost as if he didn't want to be recognized."

"How tall a man would you say he was?"

"Oh, he was very tall. Jim is, I mean, was around six feet tall and he looked small compared to the man. I would say he was maybe...six feet ten, wouldn't you Harry."

Harry Hahn nodded in agreement. Dolly stood there looking from the Frenchman to me, in turn as we spoke. Finally she butted into the conversation.

"Say, can't you talk after we've had breakfast. I'm starving," she said hooking her arms together with her two escorts.

"Yeah, let's go inside, we can talk there," the Frenchman agreed.

To be honest I really wasn't too crazy about breaking bread with the rescue mission crowd, but went along with a smile painted on my face. They had to accept me as one of them and this was just another way of cementing our relationship.

Dolly seemed to be the toast of the mission district. Everybody knew her and made over her like she was a celebrity of some kind. Although she had seen just about all of her better days, she still had an aura about her. The years had robbed her of her beauty, but to this crowd she was still the best thing around.

"Hey Dolly, two men ain't enough for you anymore; now you need three," a guy with no teeth and a nose that looked like it had exploded on his face said as we sat down at a long table.

"Hey, Popeye, it takes three to take your place," Dolly called back, getting a rise out of the men that heard her.

"Who's the new guy, Dolly; your manager?" another guy yelled.

"No he's from the IRS and wants to do an audit on last years taxes," Dolly joked.

Once we were seated the catcalls seemed to wane slightly. I wanted to pump as much information as I could out of DuBonnet while I had the chance. He was talking and I was listening.

"I didn't know Jim had a brother?" DuBonnet asked thoughtfully.

"Yeah, they didn't keep in touch. Did you know that Jim's real name was Eric Philpot?" I offered.

"That's what Dolly was saying earlier. No, I didn't know that either. That's not unusual down here though. Most of us are running or hiding from something," DuBonnet said thoughtfully and then grinned. "What do you think I'm running from?" he asked.

I sized the man up quickly. DuBonnet really didn't look like he fit down here. Oh, he had on dirty clothes and wore a two days growth of beard, but he carried himself very well. I could see him in a Brooks Brothers suit carrying a briefcase into a court room; he just had that demeanor about him. I ventured a guess.

"I'll say you left a flourishing law practice and moved down here to get away from it all," I said.

"You are a very observant man, Harley. Actually I worked for a law firm in Spokane. I fell in love with the grape and out of love with my wife and family. Actually, I preferred my drinking friends over them. My wife wouldn't drink with me, but my friends would," DuBonnet said as he looked at me with watery eyes that didn't show any sign of remorse as he talked about the past.

"Yeah, my undoing was a guy name Jack...Jack Daniels," I confessed.

"Hahn there was an engineer. He worked for Boeing until he showed up at work drunk one day and they fired him. You didn't even look for work after that, did you, Harry?"

"No. I didn't need the hassle. There's too much made out of routine; it becomes a rut and the rut becomes a grave. Now I am free to do and go anywhere I want," Harry said, sounding like so many other drunks I'd talked to in the past.

"What line of work were you in, Harley?" DuBonnet asked.

"Law enforcement," I confessed. "I was a good cop, but a better drunk. They said they didn't need a great lush and let me go. That's why Jim's brother asked me to nose around and see if I could find out anything on his brother. The trouble is it cuts into my drinking time, so I have to ask questions early in the morning before cocktail time," I said playing the role.

"A cop; I knew I smelled a cop," Hahn said with a sneer.

"I was a cop, but not now," I corrected.

"I dated a lot of cops in my younger days," Dolly cut in, "that's when I lived in Frisco; the city by the bay," she said dreamily and then started singing softly, "I left my heart, in San Francisco," before she went to the next verse she was joined in song by a short Italian looking man that still had a good singing voice, "high on a hill, it call's to me."

By this time the song had stirred up enough memories in the breakfast crowd that half the room started singing along. I felt like I was in a Rodgers and Hammerstein musical. I halfway expected the people to jump up and start dancing a choreographed routine any second.

Before they were able to finish the song the serving door was opened and they instantly stopped singing and headed for the lineup. I hung back allowing most of the occupants to get ahead of me. I watched as they received their food gratefully and headed back to where they'd been sitting earlier.

Just as Dolly got her plate of food and turned around to get her coffee, she looked towards the front of the dining hall. She did a slight double take and then caught my eye, giving her head a nod towards the man that had just entered. I didn't know what she meant and the expression on my face must have told her so, so she mouthed the word 'W-A-L-L-A-C-E.

I looked in the direction Dolly had motioned and saw a husky man in his late forties moving towards the serving line. I definitely wanted to talk to him seeing as how no one really knew under which bridge he lived.

I stepped out of line letting the guys behind me move up one space, which they did eagerly, and moved to the back of the line where Wallace was now standing. Dolly, meanwhile, had gotten her coffee and set her food and drink on the table and was walking towards Wallace and me.

"Hey, Wallace," she called out from a good ten feet away. "Where've you been keeping yourself, honey?" she said, obviously alerting me again as to the man's identity.

"Hi Dolly," I've been out of town; the Caribbean," Wallace joked.

"Oh I love St. Tropez, this time of year," Dolly smiled.

"St. Tropez is on the French Riviera," Wallace laughed.

"Oh, yeah, I keep forgetting, but they both have a lot of water nearby. I want you to meet a good friend of mine, Wallace. This fella right here, Harley Quinn; Harley, this is Wallace," Dolly said warmly.

Wallace looked at me minus the smile, "Quinn," he said seriously; then added, "He's a cop."

Dolly looked quickly at me and then back at Wallace, "He was a cop, Wallace; 'was' being the operative word here. He got kicked off the force for beating up the Chief of Police," Dolly lied, I supposed for a good reason.

Dolly knew what she was doing, because the moment she said what she did Wallace grinned from ear to ear. He looked at me like I had just saved a puppy from drowning.

"You did? Did you bust him up real good? I beat up an Assistant DA one time. I worked him over real good. I ain't ever beat me up a Chief of Police, though," Wallace said and then stuck out a hand almost twice as big as mine to shake.

"Say Wallace, glad to meet you. So you beat up an Assistant DA, huh; well that's one up on me. I ain't ever beat up an Assistant DA," I laughed.

"I'd like to give a mayor a good working over sometime. That's about as high as you can go in local government, mayor," Wallace said, obviously on some kind of revenge trip.

"Yeah, I guess about the only one that I know that did that was this really tall guy I knew once. I never knew his name but he was really tall and tough. You don't know of any really tall guys around here, do you Wallace," I said, taking a wild shot in the dark.

"I seen a really tall guy down here once; he was with Blinky. We think he might have killed Blinky. He might

55

have even killed Jim Conley, too. If I was you I'd stay away from him."

"You said you saw him with Blinky...did you get a good look at his face?"

Wallace didn't answer right away, but looked around to see if anyone was listening besides me; Dolly had already left the two of us and went back to the table.

Once he was satisfied no one could hear us Wallace spoke, "Yeah I did. I ain't told any body that I did, though, because I don't want the guy looking to do to me what he did to Blinky and Jim. I seen that guy before, but I don't know where it was," Wallace said and squeezed his eyes shut before going on. "If I think too hard it gives me a headache. I can't remember where I seen that guy before...I tried."

"Wallace, if I get a picture of that guy would you be able to identify him. If he killed Blinky and Jim I want to catch him. They were my friends. Do you think you'd recognize him again?" I asked cautiously.

"You ain't still a cop are you? I ain't helping no cop find no one."

"No, I got kicked off the force for being drunk...and beating up the Chief of Police," I quickly added.

"Yeah, the Chief...yeah, I'd know the guy's face. You get me a picture of him and I'll identify him for you," Wallace said as he looked around me towards the front of the line that had moved away from us. "I got to get something to eat," Wallace said, indicating that the talking was over and now it was time to eat.

We each got a plate of scrambled eggs and bacon and two biscuits. Wallace went to a table with some other men and I returned to the table where Dolly, Harry, and the Frenchman were just finishing up their meal.

The Frenchman spoke first, "You must have found a friend in Wallace. Usually he doesn't have too much to say to anyone, much less a stranger."

"He's never met anyone that beat up the Chief of Police, I guess," casting a quick look at Dolly who was smiling widely.

CHAPTER

7

SOMETHING WALLACE said toyed with my thoughts for sometime after I left the mission. He'd said that the tall man he'd seen with Blinky looked familiar to him. I felt fairly sure that if Wallace had seen the man down here he would definitely have been able to finger him for being a local. Maybe Wallace had seen the guy nosing around the area where he hung his hat, however; wherever that might be.

DuBonnet had also placed the man at around six feet ten inches tall. The mug books are not loaded with shots of guys that stand that tall; not ones that I'd ever seen anyway. Maybe a call to Jeff Curtis might turn up something.

I found a pay phone not too far from the mission and called my old friend and told him I was interested in the names of any local low life that stood in excess of six feet six inches tall with no cap on the other end of the ruler.

"You forming a basketball team; we already have one, haven't you heard?" Jeff joked.

"No, I didn't know that; when did that happen?"

"Are you onto something with your investigation into the skid row killing?"

"You mean killings, don't you Jeff. I think the same guy might have done both the skid row killings. Both victims were seen in the company of a very tall man shortly before their bodies were found. The more I look at the case, the more convinced I am that the same man did both jobs."

"That's funny; no one told us anything about seeing a tall man with the murdered victims. This is the first I heard about it."

"That's because you're a cop, Jeff. People down here don't talk to cops unless it's absolutely necessary. They don't see me as a cop...well, not one currently, anyway. As far as they know I'm just a drunk asking some questions about a couple of guys that got knifed."

"Hey, maybe you're on to something. I'll bring this up at our next meeting. When dealing with cases involving drunks, we'll all get drunk. D'you think the Chief will go for it?" Jeff chuckled.

"He might not, but you wouldn't have any trouble getting a lot of support from some of the guys up there."

"Do you want to swing by and pick up the info on the 'Too Tall' mug shots or do you have an e-mail address I can send them to?"

I had a computer all right, but had to drop the internet because it wasn't free. My finances being what they had been prior to the Philpot bonanza I had to make a choice of the internet or cutting out food for four days a month; I'd opted to cut the internet. I told Jeff I'd drop by and pick up the information he had for me. He said it would be ready within the hour.

ANTONIO 'PORKY' PALAZZO was a lowlife from way back. He would steal the pennies off a dead man's eyes and not think a thing about it. He had come by the nickname, 'Porky' easily enough, since he resembled Porky Pig. He had the same little ears pinned flat against his head as a pig and a nose that looked more like a pig snout than a nose. Standing five feet five in his stocking feet, and measuring about the same around the girth made 'Porky' a natural nickname.

I'd busted him once when I was with the SPD for mugging senior citizens and stealing the medications they'd just gotten from a pharmacy and then selling them back to seniors at a reduced price. Whatever he got for the drugs was all profit to him. I'd rouged him up pretty good claiming that he'd fallen down when he tried to escape after I'd cuffed him. I told him if he didn't go along with my story there would be a few broken bones the next time we met. He went along with it.

I hadn't seen Porky since that last bust six years earlier, but I'd heard he had moved up to the big time, hiring himself out as a hit man for the mob. When I first heard the news I had serious doubts about the rumor's validity, seeing as how I'd always pegged Porky for a coward that had to pick on the elderly to get his tainted money. Somehow he'd found the nerve to graduate to a clientele that was more capable of defending themselves.

As I exited my old precinct after seeing Jeff Curtis and picking up a copy of the files on guys over six feet six inches tall, I spotted Porky sitting in a parked car at the curb just ahead of my own vehicle. He appeared to be waiting for someone and never once looked in my direction from the time I'd first spotted him. His interest was directed towards the front of an apartment building located on the opposite side of the street from the police station and towards the middle of the block, or so I thought anyway.

Porky was sitting behind the steering wheel of a year old Cadillac Eldorado and wearing a sharp looking sport coat and smoking a cigarette. It certainly looked like Porky's financial status had improved, and considerably.

As I neared my car Porky tossed his cigarette out the open window and got out of his car. He was looking across the street at three men who had just driven up in a dark colored Chevrolet and were getting out. I figured it to be a couple of wise guys and their lawyer and Porky wanted to wish them well.

I had just climbed into my car, that looked like it came from 'Rent a Wreck,' when I heard the burst of gunfire behind me. I whirled around in a semi crouch and reached for my .45 which was still locked in the top drawer of my desk back at my office; the office I hadn't been to in over a week.

Porky was running back towards his car with his gun in his hand. The three guys from the Chevrolet were lying on the ground and not moving. Porky glanced in my direction but kept running until he'd reached his Cadillac. It was only then that it soaked in to his brain that he knew me. He did a quick double take and then realizing I could finger him as the shooter, began firing in my direction.

I lay down in the seat as I heard the staccato sound of the bullets as they hit the side of my car, leaving large, oblong holes due to the angle from which they were coming; some having ricocheted off the pavement. My car hadn't looked good before the shooting and the addition of bullet holes didn't do a thing to help its appearance.

Hurriedly I slid across the seat divider and opened the door on the passenger's side. I didn't know if Porky was moving in my direction or not and wanted as much metal between him and me as possible. I heard the roar of an engine and hoped, as well as assumed, it was the Eldorado. Peeking up over the edge of the door and out through the side windows of the Dodge, I saw I was right. That's when I noticed that the glass was missing on the entire left side of my Dodge.

The tires of the Cadillac squealed away from the curb sending up a plume of dark grey smoke off the pavement. I figured Porky thought I was packing heat and didn't want to chance rushing my car. I'd made it a practice not to carry my gun with me when I was under the power of JD, but now that I was determined to dry out I'd have to start carrying again.

By this time people were running out of the precinct building and the two small businesses directly across the street from it, as well as the apartment building. They were huddling around the three guys down in the street. There must have been four or five cops already there and more on the way.

I hurried to where the victims of the shooting lay and up to where Captain Jaime Bruce was bending down checking for a pulse; he didn't find one on any of the men.

"Who is it, Cap," I asked as the Captain stood up.

He gave me a quick glance before answering, "This is Rich Millsap," he said motioning towards one of the downed men, "and this man is Art Crosby, two detectives from homicide. The guy in the middle is Vito Correlli. They were bringing him in for questioning in a gangland style shooting we're investigating. He'd called and said he could give us some information on it. I had Millsap and Crosby go out and bring him in. These were two good cops," Captain Bruce said dropping his head and closing his eyes.

"Well, I saw the shooter and can ID him for you...It was Antonio "Porky" Palazzo; he tried to take me out also. He wounded the pavement and killed my car. I'll go back inside and make a statement," I offered.

"Yeah, thanks Harley; thanks...I hate this job...at least this part of it," Captain Bruce said more to himself than to me.

I KNEW EXACTLY what Captain Bruce meant and how he felt. I'd had a similar experience a few years after starting on the force and had seen my partner, Walter Kowalski, shot down in an ambush. It's always bad, but especially when you know the ones involved.

We'd gotten a call about a family disturbance in the "Little Harlem" section of town and went to investigate. When we got there both of us went up to the door and knocked. The lights were on inside, but no one answered the door. After a second knock, my partner became suspicious and told me to go around to the back of the house. I had just rounded the corner and was halfway to the back when I heard the shotgun blast behind me. I raced around to the front again only to have the shooter run through the house and out the back door and escape unseen into the night.

My partner lay there on the porch with his guts in his hands and a terrified look on his face. He was probably dead before he hit the porch floor. Because we were so close, I had the dutiful, but painfully difficult task of telling his wife that her husband had been killed in the line of duty. I never wanted to have to do that again. I believe that was one of the contributing factors to my friendship with Jack Daniels.

AFTER FILLING OUT a statement and telling my eyewitness account to the homicide boys, I headed home. As I drove along I began to have a nagging thought. If Porky Palazzo had truly recognized me as the witness to the killings, it would be greatly to his advantage for me to be silenced. It's hard to cross examine a corpse; and a written statement doesn't carry near the weight as a testimony from a living eyewitness. I'd have to keep a sharp eye out for Porky. With that thought, I decided to make a detour by my office and the desk drawer where I kept my .45 automatic.

As I headed in the direction of my office I caught myself licking my lips nervously a couple of times. I knew the next few hours were going to be rough. My body was about to start screaming for a jolt of alcohol and there was nothing I could do about it. My hands began to sweat and my mouth became dry.

I gripped and re-gripped the steering wheel as my head became warmer and warmer. When I reached over to turn the radio on I noticed my hand beginning to tremble. It was about time to face my first real test on the road to sobriety.

Have you noticed how your mind gets locked onto something and no matter how hard you try you can't seem to get it off that particular subject? That's what I started going through. I tried to think of the shooting I'd just seen, but my mind kept creeping back to Jack. I fumbled with the radio dial trying to get a talk show that would hopefully get me involved in the question of the day; I couldn't find one. Everything I tried seemed to fail. I needed something more powerful than mere thoughts right now.

"As a man thinks, so is he," I said out loud; this quote becoming my mantra.

"What is the deeper meaning to that statement," I asked aloud?

Now this may sound weird, but it's true. I hadn't read the Bible in years, but I suddenly saw another verse of scripture that was joined to the first. This verse said, "Take every thought captive."

I did a little unofficial editing of the verses of scripture and came up with my own version. "Take every thought captive, for as a man thinks, so is he." The words were powerful and not merely letters stuck together to form words in a sentence. They were loaded with 'truth.' If a person rejects the truth in anything, all they're left with is a lie. And you can't live on a lie.

As these phrases and verses invaded my mind there was a shift in my thought process. You cannot concentrate on two things at one time, and the more I concentrated on the verses the less power the thoughts of alcohol had on me. The temptation was still there, but not nearly as profound now.

I became so absorbed in my new found way of thinking that I didn't notice the car that pulled into the left lane and was moving up alongside me. If I had I would have noticed that it was a Cadillac Eldorado.

Something, but don't ask me what, caused me to glance to my left just as the Eldorado pulled even with me. I didn't recognize the car or the driver, but I certainly recognized the gun in the man's hand. Instinctively I fell to my right and hit the brakes at the same time. The bullet hit the windshield post just above the driver's side view mirror.

My sudden brake caused the tailgater directly behind me to plow into the back of my battle-scarred Dodge. Fortunately it hit a spot that had already been nailed by a tailgater six months earlier, so the damage to the damaged area was barely noticeable. The Eldorado sped away and was weaving in and out of traffic when I finally raised my head up and peered over the steering wheel.

Porky hadn't wasted any time in trying to silence the only witness that could send him away for life, namely me. I hadn't figured he would try to make a hit on me so soon. I didn't think he'd try again real soon, but I wasn't taking any chance. After all, I'd already been wrong once.

CHAPTER

8

IT HAD BEEN a long time since someone had actually attempted to kill me, and as strange as it may sound, it felt good. Not that I enjoy having someone try to blow my head off, mind you; but to be involved in something that requires sobriety to simply stay alive. This was the first time I had all my bodily cylinders clicking at one time in ages. But my cylinders also told me I needed to have a tune up by getting in shape.

Traffic was starting to back up behind me and the tailgater that had ran into the back of my car, so I did the usual fender bender thing and got out and acted as though I was concerned about the damage to my car. The other driver was looking at my car and scratching his head.

"I hope you're not going to try and tell me that I did all this?" the man said as I walked back to where he was surveying the damage to his car as well as mine.

"No, no. some of these dents were already in the car. I think this is a new one, here," I said pointing to a spot where a blotch of paint matched the color of his car.

"Hey, I'm not going to have my insurance pay for all these dents," he stated angrily and then noticing the windows on the passengers side of my car added, "I suppose you're going to claim my car did this damage also?"

I responded offhandedly, "The windows and the bullet holes, you mean? No, I just picked them up within the last hour."

The man's eyes widened and his tone of voice softened considerably, "Oh, I didn't mean anything by that wisecrack. We'll just let the insurance companies straighten it out."

"I'll tell you what, if you want to just call it even, we can. I'm not about to take my car in to get it fixed because it's still in good running condition. Unless there's a reason you want a police report on it, I'm willing to forget it."

The man smiled and rubbed the back of his neck as he thought about my offer. After he'd thought things out he answered, "Hey, it's all right with me. There wasn't that much damage done to my car and no one was injured. Thanks," he smiled.

I looked at him very seriously now, "But let me warn you about tailgating. There was no way you would have been able to keep from hitting me as close to my rear bumper as you were driving. Remember, one car length for every ten miles per hour that you're driving."

"Is that what it is? I keep forgetting the number of feet. In fact, I thought it was one car length for ever twenty miles per hour," he replied, also in a serious voice.

"You're not the only one that thinks that, believe me. The next guy you run into might not let you off the hook as easy as I did. In fact I know people that would be lying on the ground right now claiming you'd injured their back and neck," I lectured.

"I'll remember that, honest I will," he said as he started moving towards his vehicle in order to get away from me and get moving again.

I half waved to him and climbed back in my car and headed for my office. I needed my equalizer and fast. Twice now, this little creep Palazzo had tried to shoot me and he'd missed both times. If he tried one more time I wanted to be ready for him.

When I arrived at the building where my office is located I parked in a yellow zone in front and hurried up to my office. I'd just gotten my .45 and slipped it into my shoulder holster when the phone rang. I don't know who I expected; Cass maybe, or the police, but certainly not the person on the other end.

"Hello, Quinn Investigations. May I help you?" I asked easily.

There was silence on the other end, "Hello, anybody there? This is Harley Quinn, can I help you?" I repeated.

"Quinn, you're dead meat," the caller said and hung up.

I knew instantly that the caller was none other than Porky Palazzo. This call was just his way of telling me that he knew where my office was located and he could hit me anytime he had a mind to do so. He was going to have to shoot a little straighter than he had so far, though.

When the phone went dead on the other end I hung up and went back downstairs to where my car was parked. I was glad it was early September because the weather hadn't started turning cold yet and I would be able to get over to my friend Stewart Weston's place to get my car patched up without freezing to death. The only problem with Stew was that he tended to take his own sweet time about fixing my car when the necessity arose. That could be because I never had the money to pay him when he was finished and would have to pay on the installment plan. Of course, this time it would be different.

As I drove towards the town of Redmond and Stewart's singlewide mobile home, perched precariously on a sliver of ground he owned alongside the Bear, as he called it; short for Bear Creek, I ran some things through my mind.

First off, I didn't look for Porky Palazzo to stick around Seattle for too long, not knowing that I knew he was the shooter that had made the hit in front of the police station. No, not even Palazzo was that stupid. I figured that his phone call was just a parting shot to let me know he knew he was aware of who could put the finger on him.

The second thing that kept coming to mind was the size of the man that had more than likely killed Eric Philpot and Blinky. No one on the list of names that I'd gotten from Jeff Curtis even came close to fitting in with the area of town the killings had taken place in. I knew a couple of the guys on the list and they were dirty through and through, but not even near the point of living like Philpot and Blinky.

Just as I made the turn onto the narrow road that led along the creek bank towards Stewart's place I had a thought pop into my head. Football!

Have you ever had that happen when you're totally absorbed in a certain thought direction and for no reason at all another area of thought barges to the front of the line of your conscious awareness? Why would I think of football at a time like this? Then I realized why it had happened. The sign on a mailbox post I was nearing said, 'Go Seahawks.'

STEWART WESTON lived like a '60's hippy; he looked like a '60's hippy, and he talked like a '60's hippy. Stewart Weston was a pot smoking hippy from the sixties and proud of it; right down to his long, grey hair, the scraggly salt and peppered beard that was mostly salt now, tie-dyed pants, loud polyester shirt, headband, bookkeeper colored glasses, and sandals. But he could fix anything associated with cars, trucks, boats, and I suspect airplanes.

I'd been out here a number of times before and was always amazed at the place's sameness. Even the rusted out old wash tub was still in the same spot on the deck with the busted railing, as it had been two years earlier when he'd replaced a fender on my car that was interfering with the ability to make hard right turns. His speech certainly hadn't changed either.

"Say man, what's happening?" Stew said as he opened the screen door that wouldn't close all the way.

"I need some work done on my ride; a couple of windows."

"No problem, man; come on in," Stew said inviting me into his inner sanctum.

Stew's place looked like a bomb had gone off in an antique shop and everything from the Haight/Ashbury era of the '60's had landed in his yard; some of it finding its way inside his mobile home. There were posters of Jimi Hendricks, the Who, and Janice Joplin displayed proudly on the rain stained walls of the living room. I figured he'd placed the one with the Mamas and the Papas in his bedroom, along with the Who, the Beatles and the Rolling Stones.

He saw me taking it all in and asked with a smile, "So, what do you think of my new additions to my pad, man; groovy, eh?"

"Groovy, Stew; like it's the grooviest," I said holding back a laugh so hard it hurt and figuring he was referring to the posters.

"Yeah, I think it's pretty cool. So how'd your glass get blown away, man?"

"A guy didn't like the way I drove, I guess. You know, road rage," I lied.

"Hey man, that's why I don't go out much, you dig; too many hot heads on the road now days. They need to mellow out, man; like kick back and smoke a little weed and listen to some cool sounds."

"It's a jungle all right, Stew. Any idea how long it will take you to fix up the car?" I asked not wanting to push Stew too much, but wanting to get the repairs started as soon as possible.

"Let me look at it. I've got some old doors out back that still have good glass in them. Let's go see if any of them will fit," Stew grinned.

We walked out into his back yard, if you could call it that. What he called his back yard was actually the area on both sides of the mobile home. There was nothing in back but the creek bank, and it had eroded a little since my last visit.

"I think I have a couple of doors over here, man," Stewart said as we made our way through the maze of car parts strewn all over the ground. "Yeah, man, like right here. I knew I'd picked this up for a reason."

Stewart had two doors that he was able to remove the windows from and literally made them fit my car by doing a little grinding and reshaping by using a grinder and a heating device. The guy should be working in a custom auto shop somewhere instead of living out here in no-man's land, I thought to myself.

I was back in Seattle within four hours from the time I'd arrived at Stewart's pad. The car's windows were in and except for the bullet holes and the new dent in the back end, as small as it was, the car looked like it had prior to the shooting incidents.

I wanted to go back down to the mission district and ask around if anyone else had seen anything that might tie into the killings of Conley and Blinky. There were a few more questions I had for Pastor Richard and his assistant, Gus Hazifotis, as well. For instance, how long had they been preaching the gospel to the lost souls in that neighborhood? If they had been there for very long, could they remember any other knifings that might have occurred over the years?

It was a long shot, I knew, but you can never tell when you might get lucky. I didn't know it at that time, but this was my lucky day. And the luck would come from a most unusual source.

I had just parked at the curb about a half block from the mission and was getting out when a patrol car passed by. It suddenly stopped and backed up. The patrolman riding shotgun looked at me with a curious eye.

"Hey, Harley...Harley Quinn, is that you?" the man asked.

I looked at the officer that obviously knew me by name as well as by sight," Yeah, do I know you?"

"Probably not, you taught a class I attended at the junior college; 'Introduction into Law Enforcement.' I sat in the very first row; Carl Butterman."

As unlikely as it was, I did remember him. He'd been a huge question mark. Always asking the hard questions that the other students were too embarrassed to ask, or just never thought to ask them; he was the best student in the class.

"Yeah, I do remember you Butterman. I see you made it through the academy all right? What can I do for you?"

"Nothing, really; I just wanted to say hi and see what you were up to these days; that's all."

"Actually I'm working on a murder case. The drunk that got his head handed to him a few weeks back. The man's brother hired me to look into his murder."

"I'm glad to see you're still in the trade," Butterman smiled a friendly smile that seemed to say he was sincere. "I was one of the first patrolmen on the scene the night of the murder. You do mean the murder of a guy named Conley, don't you?"

"Yeah, that's the one," I replied.

"I was also on duty several weeks earlier when a guy by the name of Blinky was also knifed. I'll tell you something, I think the same guy punched both their tickets," Butterman said seriously.

"What makes you think so?"

"I take it you've heard about the guy named Blinky getting it?"

"Yeah, Pastor Richard told me about it."

"I saw Blinky not more than twenty minutes before he was found with his guts hanging out and he was walking along with...," I cut him off.

"A very tall man, right; a man that was close to seven feet tall," I said with a smile.

"How'd you know that?"

"Hey, I was a good cop, remember," I said feeling just a little bit proud of myself for being as up on this case as the police were.

"Yeah, but you'll never guess what I saw them get into," Butterman said with a wry smile?

"A pickup truck," I said taking a wild guess.

"A brand new Lincoln Continental. Now who in their right mind drives around in a Lincoln Continental picking up derelicts off a skid row street? And standing nearly seven feet tall, at that," Butterman added.

"Any dope peddlers in town that tall?" I asked.

"Nope, nearest is maybe six four. It wasn't even the kind of ride a pusher or pimp would be driving. This car was strictly straight up respectable. I think we've got some rich guy gets his kicks by knifing winos that no one will miss; well no one but other winos, that is."

I nodded in agreement, "Sounds plausible to me. Any ideas as to who it might be?"

Butterman looked around at his partner and then returned his gaze in my direction, "Might want to check out the Sonics; you know, size, type of car, and especially the background of some of them."

"Are you profiling, Butterman," I queried?

"Don't we all," he smiled as they slowly moved on down the street.

WHAT BUTTERMAN didn't say was why he hadn't checked out the Seattle Supersonics personnel. He didn't have to say it; he knew I was well aware of the leeway they give these guys. No one is going to be allowed to go questioning a bunch of professional ballplayers over the death of one or even two 'insignificant' winos that might get killed. The mayor and city council would have the players union, the NBA, the ACLU, and if you hassled any black guys, the NAACP as well as the Reverends Jesse Jackson and Al Sharpton, down on their necks if they even insinuated the killer might be a player, or a black player as the case may be.

No, there'd have to be at least two credible eyewitnesses that could positively put the player at the scene holding a knife and blood dripping from his hands before the DA would even dare touch the case.

What Butterman said, however, intrigued me. Someone as tall as the man witnesses said was in the company of both the victims just might have a tie in with the basketball team. A person pushing seven feet tall would almost have to have something to do with a basketball team; especially in a town that had a professional franchise.   Maybe I would seek a few answers from the team PR man, or better yet, head coach. It wouldn't hurt...I hoped.

CHAPTER

9

PASTOR RICHARD was busy sweeping the mission floor when I walked in. He didn't see me right away and was humming an old gospel tune I remembered from my youth.

"Swing down sweet chariot, stop and let me ride," I said, half singing and speaking the words.

The pastor turned around with a big smile on his face. "I love those old gospel tunes. They seemed to have a lot more meat to them than the praise and worship songs of today."

"They do? To be honest, Pastor, I haven't been to church in so long I don't know what they're singing now," I said honestly.

"I take it you were raised in church; am I right?"

"Oh, yeah; twice on Sunday and every Wednesday night," I smiled.

The pastor knelt down with a dust pan and swept the small mound of dust into it. He nodded with his head for me to follow him as he headed into the kitchen area where there was a large trash can near the door.

"So what brings you back down here, Mr. Quinn?" he asked.

"I wanted to know how long you have been here at the mission," I replied.

"Just under a year; I was transferred here from another mission on the other side of town. I'm kind of the troubleshooter of the ministry, you might say. Pastor Hazifotis was with me at the other mission as well. He didn't come over until he could get another assistant pastor trained in his duties at that mission. Why do you ask; is it important?'

"No, it's just that I was wondering if there'd been any killings around this time last year," I answered.

"Funny you should ask that, Mr. Quinn. Gus and I were talking just this morning about two killings last year in the district where we were serving that were somewhat similar to these. Two men were violently killed by knife wounds. In fact one of the men must have put up a valiant fight and had the palms of his hands severely cut. One of his hands was cut from the fist knuckles all the way down to the wrist bone. Horrible even to think about," the pastor said grimacing.

"I take it there were no witnesses then either, huh?"

"No, no one saw either man in the company of anyone. To be honest, I don't think they would admit it even if they had seen someone with the victims.

"Most of the people down here that are, well, let's say more in charge of their faculties, are scared to death of dying. Many of them have confided in me that they don't even like to go to sleep at night, afraid they'll die in their sleep. So they become very closed mouth when it comes to identifying someone that might come after them if they testified against that person."

I just started to make a comment when the phone rang and the pastor was forced to answer it. After giving his name to the caller, the pastor just listened. I figured he was going to be tied up with the caller for awhile so I gave him a wave, which he returned with a shrug of his shoulders and a half smile.

My next stop was to the newspaper office. I wanted to check back issues of the newspaper to see if anything like this had happened before. I checked the microfiche on old newspapers over the past five years, starting with the oldest editions.

I didn't see anything that might tie in to the recent killings until I got to the editions two years back. Five deaths had been reported in the skid row areas of the city that year. Two of the deaths were by gunshot wounds and three were by knifings. All three knifings had been committed between September and December.

When I checked the papers from the previous year I found six deaths. Two were by derelicts that stepped out in front of passing cars, one by strangulation, one by gunshot, and two by knifings. The knifings were so violent the reporter said the killer must have been a very large, very strong man. The murders were committed in November. The first on a Sunday night and the second killing occurred on a Thursday night, almost three weeks later.

When I checked the deaths of Eric Philpot; the newspaper article actually identified him as Jim Conley; I found that he was killed late Sunday night or very early Monday morning, the time being set around midnight. The article on Blinky was not very enlightening at all, other than saying his body had been found around 8 AM Monday morning.

I left the newspaper records office with a clearer picture of the person, or persons, involved in the skid row killings. With the exception of the Thursday night killing, the others had all occurred on a weekend, either late Sunday night or very early Monday morning.

When I reached my car I sat inside for several minutes pondering what all I knew about the murders of the now seven victims. I felt that all seven were connected in some way, but how? That was the sixty four thousand dollar question.

I decided to call it a day and headed for home. It took me awhile to get out of the parking lot because of the crew of stripe painters that were repainting the parking lot lines. They had closed off one side of the lot and painted it the day before and now were just finishing up the other half. With one of the exits being blocked off, traffic had backed up causing a delay.

As I sat there in my car looking down the rows of fresh painted lines I had a thought creep into my consciousness. The white lines on the black surface of the blacktop parking lot reminded me of a football referee's shirt.

The thought slowly shifted my consciousness in the direction of sports and the possibility that a professional athlete could be involved. Suddenly my mind lit up like a tall Christmas tree. Sports and what Officer Butterman had said. That was what I needed to check on; the schedule of the Seattle Supersonics.

I pulled back into another parking space and sprinted, well, walked very fast, back into the newspaper records office. The NBA had just started their season when the first killing had taken place, I happened to know that.

What I checked out this time was the sports pages of the newspaper the day of the killings as well as the day preceding them. My heart sank, there were no Supersonics games during the time of the killings. And when there were, they were away games. Then another article caught my eye.

"Seahawks Take Swan Dive!" the headlines of the article read.

"The Seattle Seahawks lost a heartbreaker to the San Diego Chargers last night, in the last ten seconds of the game. Quarterback Hasselhoff fumbled the ball when he dropped back to pass and was hit from behind by Linebacker Ted Kowalski. Cornerback Tory Sweeny picked up the loose ball and sprinted thirty nine yards into the end zone as the clock ticked down to zero. The extra point was good."

I didn't read the rest of the article, but scanned the microfiche to the next knifing date. The article on the sports page read much like the first one I'd read.

"It's dejavu all over again! For the second time in as many weeks the Seahawks are beaten in the last ten seconds of the game. This time the heartbreaker came at the hands of the San Francisco 49'ers quarterback Joe Montoya who scrambled around in the pocket for what seemed like two days before taking off and sprinting untouched into the end zone some twenty three yards away."

AGAIN, I didn't finish reading the rest of the article. I hurriedly checked all the other dates of the knifings and the subsequent killings. It was a match. When I reached the date of the killing that had occurred late Thursday night or early Friday morning, I was convinced there was a tie in between the losses of the Seahawks and the skid row killings. They'd lost that night as well.

Then I had a disturbing thought. The last game the Seahawks had played ended just like two previous last ditch efforts on the part of their opponents, but there'd been no knifing incident. At least none that I'd read about, anyway. Perhaps I was jumping to conclusions with this sports thing.

On a hunch I checked the paper the day following the last crushing defeat of the 'Hawks. I couldn't find anything even remotely connected. Still, the other killings were following heartbreaking losses. I made my mind up to do a little follow up work on this scenario before scraping the whole idea.

It was getting late so I went back out to my car and drove home. As soon as I arrived I gave Philpot a call and brought him up to date on what I'd found out. I intentionally left out the possible connection to the Seahawks win, loss record, however, for fear of coming across like a...well, a drunk.

After checking in with Philpot I called Cassandra and invited myself over for a glass of Martinelli's Sparkling Cider. I could see her smile through the phone and hear it in her voice. I was pretty proud of myself, as well.

Several times during the course of the day I'd had that weak, sinking feeling that cried out for alcohol of some kind, but every time I had that feeling I'd have a thought come to mind. "As a man thinks, so is he." That would become my mantra and I loved it. For one thing, I was thinking like a detective again.

I wanted to run this latest possible link past Cassandra and get her take on it. She'd be honest with me in her dealing with it, and if it was something ridiculous would keep it under her hat, even though she hardly ever wore one. Actually, I'd always thought she would have made a good detective. She was certainly good at seeing through phonies and liars. Her only problem was, which was fortunate for me, that she was a sucker for a drunk; namely me.

Cass worked as an executive secretary for a large savings and loan company in Seattle. She'd been with them for over ten years and pretty much had free run of the place, due to the fact she was excellent at what she did. She'd even managed to put some of my savings, when I had some, in a fund that wouldn't allow me to touch it for a set number of years. I wasn't sure of the details, though. All I knew was that it was invested in something and someday I'd be able to draw it out. As you can see, I'm a real financial genius.

I called her at her office, but they told me she had gone out to run an errand. The woman that covered for her said she'd have her call me as soon as she got back in the office. I thanked her and hung up. The moment the phone hit the cradle it rang.

"Harley Quinn Investigations, this is Quinn," I said feeling good about the introduction.

"Mr. Quinn, I hope you can help me. I've been talking to Mr. Rodney Philpot and he informed me that you are working on a case for him; is that right?" the woman's voice said.

"Yes, I am. Is there something I can do for you?"

"I certainly hope so. My name is Florence Cargill, you may have heard of me?" she said, but didn't wait for me to answer. "I would like to hire your services to locate a distant cousin of mine. He and I were very close as children and I haven't heard a word from him in over ten years. All my efforts to locate him have failed, and when Rodney, Mr. Philpot, told me you were investigating the death of his brother, I thought you might look into the whereabouts of my cousin also."

I'd heard of Mrs. Florence Cargill, all right; as well as her husband, Norval. They were one of the richest couples in the country. They'd both came from old money and when they combined the two fortunes moved into the top five of the richest families in the country.

"Hmm, I see. Where was your cousin's last known address?" I asked."

"Right here in Seattle. You see...he too is," she paused as if it were hard for her to say the words, "...a derelict."

I could barely suppress the joyful laugh that formed in my belly. I was working again, only my clientele were rich people with derelict family members they wanted investigated, or in Mrs. Cargill's case found.

Holding back the laugh I stated, "Yes, I can do some checking around and see if I can find out where your cousin is now. What is his name?"

"His name is Robert Waldorf. The last I heard he was living in a hotel, I never knew the name of it, down in the skid row district near a rescue mission. My husband went down there, but he was unable to find out the exact location of my cousin's whereabouts. To be honest, I'm not really sure he tried all that hard to find him. He never liked Robert," she said with a tone of repugnance in her voice. The distaste, however, was for her husband's attitude rather than her cousin's addiction.

"Since I'm working in that area anyway, Mrs. Cargill, I can take your case. Do you have a picture of your cousin that I could pick up from you?"

"Yes, or I could drop it off at your office since I'll be in the city for a luncheon engagement; along with a check, of course. Will five thousand dollars get me a week of your time?" she asked nonchalantly. My heart began to race.

"Absolutely Mrs. Cargill; that should be plenty of time to find out something; even if it should be that he's left the Seattle area. As far as dropping the picture off at my office, that would be fine. If I'm not there you can just drop them through the mail slot in the door," I replied as my joy at landing another client from the society page was about to overflow.

"Oh, Mr. Quinn, you have made me so happy. I know you will be discreet in your findings and keep Mr. Cargill and my name to yourself. It wouldn't please Norval in the least to have our names in the newspaper connected to the seamier side of Seattle's citizenry. I hope that doesn't sound too...judgmental?" she said thoughtfully.

"Not in the least, Mrs. Cargill; that's why we're called, 'private investigators.' We keep our client's names private as well as our findings. The way I look at it is that your business is no one else's unless it impacts them in someway," I said frowning at the thought.

"Will you keep me informed of your findings on a daily basis...the way you are doing Mr. Philpot's investigation?"

Her question told me that Philpot had obviously explained to her that I was an alcoholic and he'd issued me a warning about my drinking. It didn't bother me, though; I'd be the same way if the shoe were on the other foot, so to speak. You don't want to give a drunk a check for an amount that could keep him gassed for two months of solid drinking.

"Absolutely, I wouldn't have it any other way," I said politely.

"All right then, we'll handle it that way. If you'll take down my phone number and the address where you can mail your final report I'll give it to you," she said.

"Whenever you're ready," I replied.

She gave me her cell phone number and the address of her personal post office box. She said she'd appreciate it if I reported directly to her. I had to assume that she didn't want just anyone having access to their home;

something I certainly wouldn't blame them for; not in today's society.

We said goodbye and I felt like a million bucks. I'd really have something to tell Cassie at dinner tonight. I could already see the smile on her face when I told her the good news. Two big shot clients in a week was more than I'd ever dreamed of for my business. Maybe I was going to make a go of this investigation gig after all.

CHAPTER

10

CASSIE'S EYES widened when I gave her the good news about Mrs. Cargill hiring me to find her long lost cousin. "You mean you've already gotten a client through Mr. Philpot's recommendation?" Cass asked.

"Yeah, but I think it has more to do with me being able to identify with the derelicts on skid row than it does about my abilities as a private investigator," I said, more to get an argument from Cassandra than anything.

"Don't you dare put yourself down that way, Harley Quinn? You are a good investigator that's why you got this other job. The rich are always looking for someone they can trust to keep their names out of the news on matters that the scandal sheets would have a field day with. Mr. Philpot believes you are that kind of detective and is passing the word around to his friends. It wouldn't surprise me if you don't get a number of other investigations due to these two."

I really couldn't argue with her on that point. If the rich lock onto a person that they believe in they tend to steer a lot of business that person's way. All I could say about that was, 'keep steering.'

I treated Cassandra to a very expensive dinner at a restaurant that is not a regular haunt of mine, which pleased her immensely. When the waiter presented me with the wine list I could see Cassandra tense. Her tenseness faded quickly, however, when I looked up at the man and handed the list back to him. The smile on her face was worth the effort it took me to make that decision.

My bout with Jack Daniels and his friends, Jim Beam, and Johnny Walker, wasn't easy. It was a tag team match between them and me; three against two. I had the upper hand though, since I felt my partner in this match was the Creator. With Him on my side I couldn't lose. Every time I started to slip the verse, "I can do all things through Christ who strengthens me," would come to mind. When that thought came in the craving would begin to lessen.

Cassandra reached across the table and took my hand. Her eyes held a new found admiration for me. She actually looked like she was proud to be with me. I know I was proud to be sober enough to enjoy her company to the fullest.

"I kind of like you, Mister," Cass said in a sultry voice.

"Oh, yeah; is this the pick up line you use with all the guys you go out to dinner with?" I answered.

"Hmm, no, just the special ones that take me to fine restaurants and don't pass out on the floor between the main course and dessert," she grinned.

"When did I ever do that?" I asked.

"When *didn't* you do that?"

"I didn't mean 'pass out between the main course and dessert,' I meant take you out to a fine restaurant."

Cass laughed that lilting laugh of hers that sounds like a gentle, babbling brook. Just the sound of it brings a smile to everyone's faces that are within earshot. Everything this woman did was right, at least to me.

As we sat there holding hands on top of the table that was lit by candlelight Cass looked around the room at the

87

other diners. Suddenly she did a double take as her gaze fell on the couple at a table two removed from ours.

"What is it," I asked, noticing her reaction.

"Don't make it obvious, but look at the second table over from ours; towards the window. That's Bubba Braden, the defensive end for the Hawks. I wonder if that's his wife, I heard he just got married," Cass said.

I casually looked around the room as though merely taking in the décor and when I turned my attention in the direction of Braden realized Cass was right. It was the big defensive lineman. He dwarfed the table that he and his date were sitting at. But then again, he dwarfed everything and everyone in the room.

"You want his autograph?" I asked.

"No, don't bother them now. I'll bet he gets so tired of people bugging him for his autograph," Cassandra said, thoughtful as usual.

"You sure, honey? I won't ask him right now, I'll wait until they've finished their meal."

"No, but we might say hello; you know, just to let him know we recognized him."

Bubba Braden and his date had been seated just after we had and both our tables were served at almost the exact same time. After we had enjoyed our meals complete with strawberry cheesecake for me and Chocolate Moose for Cassandra, we set back and enjoyed one last cup of good rich coffee.

The checks for both tables arrived at the same time and after paying, both Bubba and I arose to pull the chairs out for our dates. I looked in his direction and he had glanced at me. We both smiled at one another and I nodded. As they started past our table on their way out, Cassandra and I waited to do the polite thing and let them pass.

Bubba Braden stood six feet ten inches tall and made me feel like a little boy next to him. I couldn't get over the size of this man. His hands looked like two huge hams hanging below the sleeves of his suit coat that had to have been purchased at the Very Big and Tall Men's Store. Cassandra stood wide eyed and in awe of the size of the man accompanying the petite woman that was his wife.

"Enjoy your meal, Bubba?" I asked quietly as the couple passed us by.

"Yeah, great food, eh?" he replied with a slight nod.

"Very good indeed," I replied.

Cassandra smiled at the woman who didn't return her smile, but acted somewhat stuck up. I could read Cassandra's thoughts through her eyes...'if it wasn't for him, honey, you'd be just another face in the grand stands.'

The four of us left the restaurant together and when we reached the street Cass and I followed the odd looking couple towards the parking lot. We were only about six or seven steps behind them when Bubba dropped his car keys. Stopping to pick them up allowed us to catch up to them.

"Fumble," I said jokingly.

"Don't say that, man, I'm liable to fall on them," Bubba chuckled.

"How does the team look for the game Sunday?" I ventured.

"Good, we'll have a couple of our regulars back off injured reserve. We'll do all right," he said as he picked up the keys and looked at me.

"Good luck, we'll be watching," I answered.

"Come on Bubba, I want to go dancing," the woman said in an irritated voice.

"Be right 'witch' you, Honey," Bubba said and caught up with the stiff necked woman.

Cassandra shook her head negatively as the couple moved on in the direction of the new Cadillac. Bubba unlocked the door with his remote and then hurried around to the passenger's side and opened the door for his wife. She still wore the sour look she'd adorned most of the evening.

"What a little snot," Cassandra said quietly.

I laughed.

"I'm glad you didn't say it so he could hear. I'd hate to have had to deck the guy," I joked.

Cassandra looked at me with a wry smile, "Yeah, like you decked Sergeant Gonzalez of the SPD. I don't think a few ice cubes wrapped in a bar towel would have done you much good this time, Harley."

"Hey, there were two of them, remember."

"No Harley, if you'll remember back you'll recall that you were seeing everything double that night."

"Oh, yeah...well I still say the guy had four arms."

Just then Bubba pulled out of the parking space and headed for the parking lot exit. I noticed the Seattle Seahawks bumper sticker displayed prominently on the back bumper of the Caddy. I didn't want to think about it, but Bubba Braden had the credentials to be the tall man that had been seen in the company of both the stabbing victims. I didn't say anything about that particular thought to Cassie, however.

"Want to follow them and see where they're going dancing?" I asked to see what kind of reply I'd get from Cassandra.

"Why...you want to see me pull that woman's hair out?"

"Let's go home then," I laughed.

CHAPTER

11

IT WAS GOOD waking up in the morning and being able to remember everything that had happened the night before. This sobriety thing was all right. I shaved, showered, and got dressed and realized that I was hungry. I hadn't been in the habit of eating food for breakfast, usually just a Bloody Mary or a Screwdriver. Even drunks need their vitamins.

I went down to my favorite coffee shop which, unlike the restaurant Cass and I had dined at the night before, had a menu that I was able to translate with no problem. Bacon and eggs were simply listed as that; wonderful idea; that's what I ordered.

I picked up the complementary morning paper off the counter and opened it up. The headlines floored me.

Stabbing Victim Found Behind Bar!

The story was about the dead body of a man that had been found buried under some trash in a vacant lot in back of Rico's Bar in the mission district of town. The man's throat had been cut and the coroner estimated he'd been dead for around four days before his body had been found. The police would not comment on whether they thought the killing was by the same person that had committed the other two murders.

The article did not give the victim's name pending notification of the man's family. I'd have to give the boys down at the precinct a call and see if I could pick up any information they had neglected to tell the reporters.

Making a quick calculation on the timeline set by the coroner's office, if this was another killing like the other two, it would fit in with a the last Seattle loss. I suddenly had a thought. Had other cities had similar killings as these here in Seattle? I had to lay my hands on a Seahawks schedule.

My waitress poured me a second cup of coffee while I was absorbed in the newspaper article. When she passed by my place at the counter again I hailed her.

"Wanda, you wouldn't happen to have a Seahawks football schedule handy would you?"

"Oh sure, Harley, I carry one of every team around in my pocket," Wanda wisecracked.

"I mean hanging on the wall in the kitchen or somewhere," I grinned.

"Actually we do, Harley. What do you want to know?"

"I just want to check out who they've played and whether it was a home game or an away one."

"Just a minute, I'll bring it out to you," Wanda said nonchalantly.

She went into the kitchen and returned shortly with a small schedule. "Pete said this was an extra one he had; it's yours."

"All right, thanks Wanda. Tell Pete I owe him one," I said as I took the schedule.

"What about me; I got it for you," Wanda said, acting injured.

"Okay, I owe you, too," I smiled, "I'll take care of you the same time I take care of Pete."

"That means I may as well forget ever receiving something for my good natured-ness, then."

"You're too cute, Wanda."

I looked at the schedule and was thankful that Pete had already done a major portion of my work for me. He had posted the scores of each game next to the opponent's name. If it was a home game, the name of the home team was in capital letters. According to what Pete had here, the only other game the 'Hawks' had lost was an away game; Kansas City.

AFTER BREAKFAST I went to my old precinct to talk to Jeff Curtis. I asked him if he could run a check for me on any knifing homicides in the Kansas City area on the date the Chiefs had played the Hawks; specifically in the skid row area; or as it is more commonly referred to nowadays, the mission district. I didn't tell Jeff the reason for that particular date.

Jeff told me to grab a cup of coffee and he'd have the information in a few minutes. I grabbed a cup of coffee from the table where the pot was kept, along with a donut, and took a seat next to Jeff's desk. I was just licking the sugar off my fingers when Jeff returned.

"Here you go, Podna," he said, as he handed me two sheets of paper.

"Thanks, Jeff. I owe you again. What do you say we get out and baptize a few golf balls one of these days; my treat of course," I said taking the papers.

"You back to playing, are you?"

"I'm getting there. I have a new motto, "As a man thinks, so is he.""

Jeff pondered my words for a few seconds, "That's interesting. Whatever a person dwells on they'll eventually become, huh? Hmm, that's very interesting, indeed."

"Yeah, for the longest time I thought of myself as a drunk, so what do drunks do; they drink. Now I'm thinking of myself as a detective, so I...detect."

"A killer's thoughts are eventually carried out. That could be where the old adage, 'Take a thought and run with it,' came from; do you think?"

"Yeah, but I have a better answer than that, because that thought can lead you to trouble. I'd rather think of, 'Take every thought captive.' When you capture a thought you interrogate it to find out whether it's a good thought or a bad thought; if it's a good thought, keep it. If the thought's a bad one throw it out."

"Interesting," Jeff nodded in agreement. "That goes along with a report I was reading the other day about a 'brain storming' symposium that the top brain specialists and surgeons from around the world held in Stockholm, Sweden. The report said that one of the things they were in complete agreement about was the fact that the human brain is incapable of creating thought. They agreed one hundred percent that the brain can only receive thoughts; much like a radio receives sound waves. The question that wasn't talked about, and one I'd have asked is, 'where do the thoughts come from?"

"I think I know the answer to that question; and you probably do too," I grinned. "You attended Sunday School didn't you?"

Jeff nodded a silent agreement.

"So, what do you have on the body found in back of the skid row bar?" I asked, changing the subject.

"Not a lot, Harley. It looks like another killing by the same man, though. A very violent knife wound to the jugular vein that almost took the man's head off. Whoever the killer is, is one strong dude, I'll tell you that."

Jeff paused, "That's the reason for the info on any killings in the Kansas City area, huh?"

"Yeah, but I'm just playing a hunch. If there's anything that I find that you boys might be interested in I'll let you know personally," I said sincerely.

"I'd appreciate it. Those killings aren't getting very much attention around here. We're swamped with other cases and the skid row scene gets the back burner."

"That's pretty much always been the case in police circles. Kind of like, what people won't do for a bottle."

Jeff didn't say anything but I could see the question in his eyes. Was I speaking from personal knowledge on that subject? I didn't embellish the statement at all.

Wanting to pry as much information out of Jeff as I could, I went on, "Have you identified the victim yet?"

"No, not yet we haven't. He didn't have any ID on him although he was carrying a wallet with four dollars in it. No credit cards, naturally. The only thing he had was an old photograph wrapped so it wouldn't get torn to bits. It was of a young boy and a girl. The photo looked too old to be a picture of his kids, though. We think it might be a picture of him and maybe a sister," Jeff said and then looked around the immediate area as he said quietly, "Would you like a copy of it?"

"Yeah, I would, Jeff; if you can swing it?"

"Here you go. I made a copy just in case you stopped by. I figured if you were still working on the other murder case you might be interested in this. How's the other case going, anyway?" Jeff asked as he opened his desk and handed me a copy of the photo he'd had made.

"It's making a little headway. Like I said before, when I get enough solid info for you boys I'll cut you in on it. Right now, though, I don't have anything solid."

Jeff and I talked a little longer and I left.
When I got to my car I read the report Jeff had gotten for me on Kansas City homicides on the date in question. There had been two homicides committed over that entire weekend. As I read the report my pulse rate increased a little. The first homicide I read about was the shooting of a liquor store clerk in a robbery, and the other was...bingo; the knifing of a derelict.

I clapped my hands together with glee, like a gold miner hitting a rich vein. This couldn't be a coincidence. I knew it couldn't. And especially when I read the details Jeff had acquired on the killing. The coroner figured the killer to be a very tall man, and very strong due to the angle of the knife wound and the savagery with which the man had been knifed.

I sat there in my car for several minutes contemplating the situation. If this was what it looked like, I would have to move very carefully. The 'city fathers' don't take kindly to people involving money making concerns for their city in scandals. You can go after some groups of people, but don't mess with the ones that bring in a lot of dollars to the public treasury. And one thing was for sure; the Seahawks brought dollars to the city coffers. My next stop; the Sky Dome!

CHAPTER

12

I **CALLED the Seahawk's office and told them** my name and the nature of my business; that I was investigating a homicide and would like to talk to the head coach. The young woman was hesitant to even put me through to his office, but when I informed her that he could either talk to me or to the police, she patched me through.

"This is Coach Rawlings, how can I help you," the head coach said gruffly.

"Coach, my name is Harley Quinn. I'm a private investigator looking into several murders that have occurred recently here in the Seattle area and I was wondering if I might come out and talk to you?"

"Me; why do you want to talk to me in connection with some homicides?" the coach asked, the gruffness subsiding slightly.

"I'd like to ask you some questions about some of your players or staff," I replied.

"Look, Mr. Quinn. The last thing I need right now is someone upsetting my players and getting them off our task at hand. We've still got a good shot at making the playoffs and I don't want to do anything that might be a distraction for my players. Can't this thing wait until the playoff picture is settled?" the coach said as though very perturbed at my requested intrusion.

"Yes, Coach Rawlings, I guess it could, but are you willing to guarantee me that another killing won't take place in the meantime?"

"How could I guarantee something like that? No, I won't guarantee anything."

He paused for several seconds as he contemplated his decision.

"If you would rather the police talk to you we can arrange that," I said, hoping to help him make up his mind.

"No, no. I definitely don't want the police nosing around here; that would really be a distraction. Look I'll see you, but I don't want you bothering my players, okay?" he finally said resignedly.

"Okay, you may be able to give me all the information I'll need for the time being. When would be the most opportune time for us to meet?"

"Let's see...how about twelve thirty? I'm free for about forty five minutes. Yeah, come on out and be here around twelve thirty. I'll leave word with security; they'll tell you how to get to my office."

"Thank you, Coach. I really do appreciate..." that was all I had time to say before he hung up on me.

Oh, well, at least I would get to talk to him.

I checked my watch and saw it was only ten forty-five. I wanted to catch Pastor Richard before the noon meal at the mission was served, so I had plenty of time. I even had time to swing by my office and pick up the envelope that Mrs. Cargill had left for me, if she'd gotten there yet.

When I got to my office I found that Mrs. Cargill had been there. I opened the large envelope and removed the check for five thousand dollars, securing it into my ever growing, fat wallet. I'd glanced at the picture she'd included. I'd look at it closer when I got down to the rescue mission. I made it down there in fifteen minutes.

I took the photograph out of the envelope and looked at it before sticking it into my coat pocket. The photo of Robert Waldorf made me think of the old actor, David Niven, but when he was a young actor. Waldorf had a neat, narrow moustache and slightly curly hair that appeared to be a dark brown with graying temples.

Upon entering the mission I realized I had gotten there before lunch was served, but not before the sermon was preached. The pastor was in the middle of it, so I took a seat on the back row. If he noticed my presence he didn't let on. He was in the middle of making a point. I listened with interest.

"...You are here today, not by chance, but by appointment. Some of you may be here for the food in order to feed your body. Others of you are here for the Word of God which feeds your soul and spirit. Your body is going to die someday; but your soul and spirit is eternal.

"How many of you here today believes he or she is perfect? Could I see your hand, if you think you are perfect?" the pastor asked.

A couple of hands went up; whether the men knew what the question was is debatable.

The pastor smiled, "You think you are perfect, George?"

George looked around at the others sitting with their hands in their laps before answering, "Oh, I misunderstood the question, I guess. I put my hand down," George said, slurring his words badly.

Several people chuckled. The pastor looked at the other man with his hand raised.

"Doyle, you think you are perfect?" Pastor Richard asked.

"Yeah Pastor, pretty much so.

"I see; so you are saying you have never sinned then, is that right?"

"You didn't say that. You said did any of us think we were perfect; I think I'm perfect," Doyle replied.

"You can't be perfect if you have ever sinned. So, have you ever sinned?"

"Oh, I've sinned a few times, but I'm still perfect."

"Are you married, Doyle?"

"Yeah, I have a wife, but I don't see her that often."

"If I talked to her, would she say you are perfect?"

"Oh, don't ask her, Pastor; she doesn't think I'm perfect," Doyle said seriously.

Everyone laughed; everyone but Doyle, that is. He looked around like he didn't know why they were laughing.

A very old, weathered man sitting just in front of me raised his hand. The pastor looked in his direction and asked him what it was he wanted.

The old man replied, "Does God allow imperfect people into heaven, Pastor?" he asked seriously.

"No, Wesley, he doesn't. God's standard is perfection. There can be no imperfection in heaven."

"Then I'm a goner," Wesley replied.

"That's the good news of Jesus Christ, Wesley. When we place our trust in His death for our sins and in His resurrection from the dead, and confess that belief with our mouth, we are made perfect in God's sight."

"That's it? That's all we have to do? That sounds too easy, Pastor. What about my drinking problem?"

"Wesley, it is just that easy, but you have to mean it and believe it with all your heart. Now as far as your drinking goes, you don't have a drinking problem; I've seen you drink a pint of wine without spilling a drop. No, what you have, Wesley is a *thinking* problem. Christ can change your thinking if you'll allow Him to," Pastor Richard said, which really caught my attention.

"God speaks to us through our thoughts. When we are thinking good thoughts; thoughts about love, caring for others, helping our brothers and sisters, anything that is beneficial to us and to others, those thoughts are from God, because they are good.

"But Satan can also enter our mind with bad thoughts. Anything that is hurtful or harmful to us or to others is from Satan. So we must weigh each thought to see who that thought is coming from; the One that loves us, or the one that hates us. And believe me when I say that Satan hates us for the simple fact that God loves us.

"What does the Scripture say, 'For God so loved the world,' let's change that to, 'For God so loved Wesley, that He gave His only begotten Son, that whosoever, believes in Him shall not perish, but have everlasting life.' Wesley...Christ died in your place! Now isn't that good news? "

Wesley began to weep. His sobs came from way down deep in his soul. His little shoulders hunched up and down as the tears poured from his eyes. Others that were watching Wesley began to shed tears as well. There was a pouring out of years of guilt from a number of the people in that room. Dirty, grimy hands were slowly raised upwards all around the room as tears streamed down old, tired, wrinkled faces. Even Doyle was weeping and holding up his hands much like a little child wanting their father to pick them up.

I couldn't believe my ears. All of this was exactly what I'd been thinking about and now I was getting a second confirmation to those thoughts. The first had come from Jeff Curtis and now this one from the pastor.

Pastor Richard didn't say anything. There was nothing to say. These people were experiencing a visit from the Holy Spirit and the pastor knew that it was in God's hands now. The pastor stepped off the raised platform and moved amongst the people, stopping and praying with each one. The scene was moving to say the least. I didn't want to bother the pastor now, so I moved towards the kitchen and Geri Munoz.

Ms. Munoz was busy cooking up a healthy looking lunch for the free lunch crowd. When she saw me she smiled brightly and spoke.

"Well, what brings you back to the neighborhood?"

"Hi, I just had a quick question I was going to ask the pastor, but I don't want to bother him right now. I think he's closing a few deals out front," I answered. "I thought you might be able to help me on this," I said as I reached in my pocket and showed her the photograph of Robert Waldorf.

Geri looked at it for a few seconds and made a quizzical face. She held the photo away from her and then brought it closer like someone that is having trouble with their nearsightedness and then their farsightedness.

"Hmm, I don't know for sure, but it could be?" she said more to herself than to me.

"What is it? Do you know this man?" I hoped.

"This photo must have been taken some time back, because I would swear that this is Blinky before he hit bottom, of course," Geri said still looking closely at the photo.

"Blinky? Did you ever hear him use the name Robert or Bob Waldorf, by any chance?" I asked, only halfway hoping to get a favorable answer.

"No, no, I can't say as I did...wait a minute...Waldorf? You know, Mr. Quinn, when people used to ask Blinky where he was staying, he would laugh and say, 'Oh, I'm staying at the Waldorf Astoria,' and then he'd laugh. Why? Was that Blinky's real name, Robert Waldorf?"

"If the man in this photo is the same man you knew as Blinky it was his real name, yes. At least you've given me something to go on. Thank you so much for your time."

I said goodbye and went back to my car. Ms. Munoz had given me plenty to work with by her thoughts on just who the man in the photograph might be. At least I had something somewhat solid to follow up on. It might require another trip to see Jeff Curtis, but I was sure he wouldn't mind.

THE SECURITY GUARD at the door of the Seahawks' state of the art training facilities gave me a 'Visitors' badge and directed me to the coach's office. It was pretty much what you'd expect a head coach's office in the NFL to look like; if you have an active and expensive imagination. I know I was impressed. The coach's secretary had me take a seat until the coach was free. I picked up a Golf Digest before sitting down to wait.

After about five minutes the door opened and Bubba Braden walked out with coach Rawlings. When they looked in my direction Bubba did a slight double take. On the second glance he smiled widely.

"Hey, the guy from the restaurant last night; how're you doing," he said in a friendly tone.

The coach looked in my direction with a frown, probably thinking I had been hassling one of his star players with some of my questions.

"Yeah, that was a great meal. The veal scaloppini was delicious," I grinned.

"Hey, that's what I had too. It was great wasn't it," Bubba agreed.

The coach looked back towards Bubba, "Anyway, Bubba, that's what I think we should do come Saturday. Seal off that corner on those short passes to the outside."

"That'll be a new twist. I doubt they'll know how to handle that, all right."

"I'll talk to you about it later and we can go over a few new schemes I've worked up," Coach Rawlings said.

"Sure thing, Coach; I'm going to the weight room and then having lunch," Bubba replied, then looking at me added, "Take care."

"Same to you, Bubba, and good luck on the upcoming game with Dallas," I said, letting him know I knew the team's schedule.

THE COACH sat across the desk from me and drummed the eraser end of a pencil on his desk top as he stared at me from under firmly knitted eyebrows.

"So you think these killings coincide with games that we lose? Do you realize how that sounds? It's like you're saying we have a killer on our team; I resent that," the coach snapped.

"I didn't say I suspected someone on your team, necessarily, but I think it could be someone that travels with the team. Kansas City had the same kind of killing when you lost to them earlier this season," I explained. "The fact that the man seen in the company of the victims was a very big man and not a regular in the mission district tells me he could very easily be from one of the cities ball teams. Since the murders occurred on the nights the Hawks lost it points towards someone connected to your team."

"It could just be some sick football fan, too," the coach argued.

"Yes, but the fact that there was a murder in Kansas City after your loss there, tells me it very well could be someone that's traveling with the team on away games."

Coach Rawlings shook his head as he pondered my statement. "Yeah, I see your point. The truth is though, that I don't think it's any of my players because of our strict curfew rules when we're away. The other coaches and I watch them like 'hawks,' no pun intended. We make sure they are in bed by curfew and that we all ride to the airport on the team bus."

"The killings have occurred after the games, so curfew wouldn't be anything I'd be concerned about. No, it would be someone that disappeared after the games; someone that might have missed one of those bus rides to the airport. Have you had any incidents like that?"

The coach thought for several seconds before answering. When I saw his eyes widen just a little as though he'd thought of something, I was quick to question him.

"Did you think of something?"

"It may be nothing, I don't know. On our trip to Kansas City we were held up at the airport for about thirty minutes because of a problem with our luggage. I asked for a reason but was given the runaround so I let it drop and just waited until they'd gotten the problem straightened out."

"And you never did learn what the reason for the hold up was?" I questioned.

"No, but I can tell you this. Every one of our players was on that plane. We'd counted noses a couple of times. My last count came when they announced we were ready for takeoff," the coach stated emphatically.

"What about equipment personnel? Have you had any problems with them missing flights or being late?"

"No, the only time that happens is if one of the players or team personnel have family in or near the city we're playing then they're allowed to take a flight out the next day, but none of our players had any relatives in or around Kansas City."

"None of the players did, huh? What about staff members?"

"No, not that I remember; but I'll tell you what I'll do; I'll check with my assistants," Coach Rawlings said sincerely.

"One last question and I'll get out of your hair. Have any of your people, players or staff, been arrested for any acts of violence?" I queried.

"Mr. Quinn, you're talking about a bunch of football players. These guys play one of the most violent games in sports. Of course some of them have been arrested for acts of violence. We have one guy that threw his live-in girl friend out of a second floor window. Another picked a fight with three guys in a bar and kicked the stuffing out of all three. Another...do you want me to go on?" he grinned.

"Silly question," I answered rather embarrassedly. "I guess I'd have to rephrase that as any 'felony' convictions?"

"No, none, not anymore; we had one guy last year, but he's with another team now. He was arrested for felonious assault, but the charges were later dropped all together."

"I see. Well, if you think of anything else would you give me a call at this number," I said giving him my business card.

"Will do, Quinn; and if you'd like to talk to any of my assistants feel free to do so," the coach said as he stood up and offered his hand.

I shook his hand and thanked him for his cooperation. We said goodbye and I turned to go. That's when I noticed the team photograph on the office wall. It had everyone from the players to the coaches to the equipment manager to the towel boy.

"Say, Coach, would it be possible for me to get a copy of this picture?" I asked hopefully.

"Yeah, we have a ton of them. Just a minute, Quinn," the coach said and hit the intercom button.

"Sandy, would you bring me a couple of copies of the team photo," Coach Rawlings asked.

"Right away, Mr. Rawlings," Sandy said.

The coach looked at me, "I can't get her to call me by my first name or just 'coach.' She insists on calling me Mr. or Coach Rawlings."

"Sounds like a very professional secretary," I nodded.

"She is that, all right."

Just then the door opened and Sandy came in with the team photo. She handed them to Coach Rawlings and he handed them both over to me.

"In case you know someone else who'd like to have a photo," he smiled.

"Thanks, Coach, I know just the little girl to give it to," I said, thinking of Cassandra.

I thanked the coach again for his cooperation and headed back towards my office. There were some things I wanted to go over about the two cases I was now working on and that was the best place I could think of. It was just after I'd left the Seahawks' parking lot that I noticed a car pull away from the curb and begin following me, but staying about three cars back at all times. When I got a good look at it in my rearview mirror I realized it was a Cadillac Eldorado.

CHAPTER

13

I **WATCHED the Eldorado with a cautious eye.** I wanted to know its whereabouts at all times. No more did I want to play, 'Bullets, bullets, who's got the bullets.' Maybe I had miscalculated the stupidity of Antonio Palazzo. Maybe he didn't have the brains to get out of the city where he was the hottest thing since John Dillenger. If he had been tailing me, though, this was the first I'd noticed.

I began to slow down enough for cars behind me to pull out and go around. It wasn't long before I saw the Eldorado pull out into the left hand lane as well. This time I would be ready. I pulled my pistol from my shoulder holster and waited, watching the Caddy in my side view mirror.

When the car pulled up alongside I was ready to slam my brakes on if the need arose. It didn't. My would-be assassin was a gray haired lady with a poodle riding shotgun. I breathed a sigh of relief.

When I arrived at my office I put on a pot of coffee and laid out everything I had on my two skid row cases. I looked at Jim Conley's case first. I was a lot closer to knowing something about Conley's killer. I was sure the man had something to do with the football team. Now, I had a photo that might actually have the killer in it. And I had an eye witness that could definitely identify the man that he had seen with Blinky; Wallace. That would be the first thing on my agenda for the next day. Once I had an ID on the man with Blinky, or Robert Waldorf if that's who he was, I could then work towards placing that same man at the scene of the other killings.

Something about Geri Munoz's identifying the photo of Robert Waldorf didn't set well with me. She had taken quite a bit of time in saying who the man in the photo looked like. Maybe it was just my imagination, but I wasn't fully convinced that Blinky and Robert Waldorf were one and the same. I didn't know it at the time, but that would be cleared up the next day also.

I'd been in the office long enough to drink three cups of coffee when my phone rang. Because I was so deep in thought it actually made me jump when it rang.

"Hello, Harley Quinn Investigations," I answered.

"Hello, honey," Cassandra's welcomed voice said, but I thought sounded a little tense.

"Hi, babe, what's up?"

She paused just long enough to tell me something wasn't quite right, "Could you please come over here, Harley. I need you to help me hook up the DVD player I just bought today."

"Sure thing. I'll be there in..." I paused. It was only two thirty. What was she doing home so early? "...in thirty minutes."

"Okay, honey, I'll be waiting," she said and hung up abruptly.

I hung up with a huge question mark etched into my brain. What was Cass trying to tell me? She'd said something that didn't ring true, but what? It was also her voice; I could hear the tenseness in it.

Suddenly it hit me. I knew that something was wrong. Cassandra had a DVD player that she'd bought four days ago, but hadn't hooked up yet. I'd promised her

I would do it, but we kept forgetting to do it when I was over there. So, why did she say the DVD player she'd bought that day?

CASSANDRA'S APARTMENT was located on the fourth floor of the five story apartment building. It was one of the older but well maintained apartment buildings and had a number of fire escapes that was accessible through a bedroom window or from the hallway on each floor. Rather than go up to the front door, I had a feeling I should use that fire escape. If nothing was up, there would be nothing to worry about; she'd get a good laugh out of it. If something was up, I'd have the element of surprise on my side.

I hurried over to Cassandra's place and rang the buzzer on the secured entrance which signaled her to unlock the door from her apartment. After a couple of seconds the door lock unlatched and the electronic controlled door swung open. Rather than take the elevator I hurried out the back exit to where the fire escape that led up to her bedroom window was located. I jumped up and grabbed onto a strap attached to the bottom rung of the fold up ladder and pulled it down.

Climbing up the stairs as fast as I could without exhausting myself, I went to the third floor and climbed through the hallway window. I went to the elevator and pushed the button. When the elevator arrived I reached inside and punched the fourth floor, then stepped back as the elevator doors closed.

I hurried back out the hallway window to the fire escape and went on up to the fourth floor. I walked along the escape to Cassandra's window and looked in to make sure no one was inside. When I saw the room was empty I prayed that the window was unlatched; my prayer was answered. I quietly raised the window and climbed through.

Tiptoeing across the room to the door I opened it ever so slowly until I was able to see across the living room to the front door. Standing at the door and peering through the peephole was a man holding a gun in his right hand. Cassandra was sitting on the sofa with her hands and feet bound and a gag over her mouth.

It didn't take a super cop to figure out who the man with the gun was; Antonio Palazzo. I didn't know how he'd placed Cass and me together, and right now that wasn't important. What was important was taking him out without putting her in harm's way. The pistol he was holding was pointed in her direction.

I knew that the moment I entered that room there would be a shootout. I had the upper hand because I was facing him and he didn't even know I was in the apartment. I wanted his attention diverted away from Cass, however, and towards the other side of the room.

A vase on Cassandra's chest of drawers provided me with just what I'd need. I picked up the vase and slowly opened the door again. Palazzo was still watching the hallway. This time when I opened the door Cassandra saw me and looked from me towards Palazzo and then back in my direction. I stuck my arm through the open door and tossed the vase towards the opposite wall from where Cass was sitting.

When the vase shattered against the wall, Palazzo whirled around and aimed the gun in the direction of the noise. I shot three times hitting the man with each shot. He dropped like a fifty pound sack of Russet potatoes. Antonio "Porky" Palazzo was dead.

I hurried to where Cass was and took the gag out of her mouth and then removed the bindings from her hands and feet. While I did that, Cassandra was busy filling me in on what had happened.

"When I went to lunch today this man got in the elevator at the same time. He stuck that gun in my ribs and said if I didn't go along with him quietly he would kill me. When I looked into his eyes I believed him.

"He made me drive him here and call you, but we couldn't reach you until you finally picked up the phone. I was scared to death that you might just pop in like you usually do and he would kill you when you did. He said he knew you from way back and owed you plenty; is that right?" Cass said, her words coming staccato style, fast and furious.

Before I could answer she went on, "He said once he'd silenced you he'd be home free, whatever that means. Is he the one that tried to kill you the other day?"

Again she didn't give me time to answer as she continued on in her adrenalin rush, "He's the one that killed those two policemen and that other guy in front of the police station, isn't he?"

"Stop," I yelled! "Take a breath before you hyperventilate. Yes, yes, and yes to your questions. Yes, he owed me for busting him years ago; yes, he is the one that killed the two policemen and the informant in front of the police station; and yes, he is the one that tried to kill me. But he can't hurt anyone now. You just sit there and I'll make you some tea," I said, knowing that was what usually relaxed her.

Before I made the tea for her, I called 911 and told the operator what had happened and to send the police and an ambulance to Cass's address. Once I'd hung up the phone, I put a teakettle on and made Cass a cup of tea. By the time the water was hot I could hear the sirens and by the time Cass took the first sip of the tea, the police had arrived.

I told the policemen what had happened and Cassandra filled them in on how Palazzo had kidnapped her from work. They informed me that there was an APB out on Palazzo for the murder of the two cops Millsap and Crosby as well as Vito Correlli. Before long the place was overrun with police and paramedics.

BY THE TIME the police had taken care of all their business both Cassandra and I were exhausted from the ordeal. All she wanted to do was go to bed and get some sleep. Rest is what I needed to, so I kissed her good night and headed for my place.

When I got home I called Rodney Philpot and filled him in on my findings. I didn't tell him about Palazzo because it didn't pertain to the case he had hired me to work on. It isn't the best thing for business when someone thinks they're paying you for time spent being involved in another case. I know I wouldn't like it.

I had just hung up the phone with Philpot when it rang again. It was Captain Jaime Bruce. I was very surprised to be getting a call from him. He wanted to thank me for making his job easier in finding and doing Palazzo in. He said it would have been good if I could have taken him alive, but under the circumstances that would have been a near impossibility. We talked for a few more minutes and then he dropped a bomb on me.

"Harley, I hear that you talked to the head coach of the Seahawks today. He says that you were there to talk to him about doing an investigation on members of the team; is that right?"

"Yeah, I explained to him that the killings were all after the team had suffered a heartbreaking loss. I also told him that I wouldn't upset the team members since they were so close to making the playoffs. Why? Did he call the Chief?" I asked.

113

"No, he called the mayor and the mayor called the chief and the chief called me. They want you to promise that you'll not do anything that might upset the team's chances at making the playoffs. Will you do that?"

"I'll tell you the same thing I told Coach Rawlings, Jaime. If you'll promise there won't be any more skid row killings if the team should lose again," I said firmly.

"Harley, I have to warn you that officially we're still working on the skid row killings. I could order you off the case because you're interfering with an on going police investigation. You know I could do that," the captain said firmly, but in a civil tone.

"Yes, and I could tell you I'm not investigating those murders, but rather trying to locate a man by the name of Robert Waldorf," I stated.

"Robert Waldorf, where have I heard that name before?"

"I don't know where you might have heard it, but it belongs to a first cousin of Mrs. Florence Cargill's," I replied.

"Not 'the' Mrs. Cargill, Norval Cargill's wife," Jaime asked?

"The same," I answered.

"You're working for them, now? Boy, you believe in working for the top names on the society page, huh?"

"Yeah, who would have ever 'thunk' it, huh? I'm more surprised than anyone, believe me."

"Hey, when you've got it play it to the hilt."

"I will, you can be sure of that."

Jaime paused and took a deep breath, "Well, listen Harley just go easy on the team, will you? I'll tell the mayor that I talked to you and I'm satisfied that you're not going to do anything to make the team go flat."

"Good, oh one other thing Jaime; tell the mayor that although these derelicts may not be the upper crust of the city that he's used to rubbing elbows with; some of them still vote. And some of them three or four times in each election," I said, due to the fact the mayor had been accused of election fraud, although the charge had never been proven. I then added, "And if I find out anything concrete I'll let you know right away."

"I hope so, Harley. I'll forget the crack about the voting practices of some of our less fortunate, however."

THE NEXT MORNING I was up bright and early and called Cassandra to see how she was doing. She had called her office and told them she wouldn't be in that day because of the ordeal she'd been through the day before.

I asked her if she'd like to meet me for breakfast and she said she'd love it. I told her to meet me at our favorite breakfast place; a place called 'Just Breakfast' because that was all they served; but they served it until two in the afternoon.

When I pulled into the small parking lot alongside the diner I saw Cass's car parked near the entrance. I walked inside and as soon as Cass spotted me she waved. She looked beautiful. I was one blessed man to have her in my life.

"My you look handsome, Mister," Cassandra said with a hungry look.

"I know; it's a curse I have to live with," I replied coyly.

"And you're so modest, also," Cass said with a laugh.

Just then the waitress came up and poured me a cup of coffee and then gave Cass a refill. When I raised my eyes from the coffee cup, I found myself looking at a very tall man sitting at a table against the wall. Although the man was seated I could tell he was very tall by how he towered over the table; and it was not a small table.

CHAPTER

14

I T'S A FACT that most murder victims know their killer, but I didn't think that was the case with the victims involved here. It was my belief that the victims had just met the killer and when he offered to buy them a bottle went along with him more than willingly.

Jeff Curtis had gotten me a copy of a photograph of the victim known as Blinky and they were still trying to make a match of fingerprints and DNA results for an identity. It seems that Blinky had done an excellent job of hiding just who he was; although I had a sneaky suspicion he was Robert Waldorf.

Jeff had also gotten me a copy of a photograph of the latest murder victim. I'd swung by police headquarters and picked the photos up. Sitting in my car and going over them I ran across something interesting about Blinky. He had a tattoo on his right bicep.

The tattoo was a picture of a small skunk inside a heart outline in red. This could be a key for identifying him as the cousin of Mrs. Cargill. She hadn't said anything about a tattoo, but if she knew of one this could be major.

I called her at the number she had given me. The phone rang four times before she picked it up. She was excited to hear what I'd found out about her cousin.

"Mrs. Cargill, I may have a lead on Robert, but I'll need to ask you a couple of questions," I said.

"Go ahead, Mr. Quinn. What is it you would like to know?"

"Do you know if he had a tattoo on his right bicep?"

There was silence on her end of the line as she pondered my question. After giving it some thought, she answered, "No, Mr. Quinn. Not that I can recall. But now that you mention it I do recall that when my husband went down there to try and locate Robert he said something about the hotel where he was supposed to be staying at being next door to a Tattoo Parlor. What is it you've found out about Robert, anything?"

"I'd really rather not say right now; not until I'm absolutely sure. I should know more by the end of the day, though. I'll call you tonight and let you know what my findings are. Is that all right with you?"

"Oh, yes. I will be free all night. It will be so nice to stay home for an evening. Charity functions are so tiring," she sighed.

I assured her again that I'd call her that evening and hung up. My next stop was the rescue mission to show the Seattle Seahawks photo to everyone I could down there and see if I could find someone that might recognize a face in the photo. It was worth a try. If I was barking up the wrong tree, I wanted to know it.

The Frenchman looked at the Seahawks team photo and studied each face carefully. Taking his time, he slowly nodded his head negatively as his eyes moved from one man to the next in the photo. Finally with a shake of his head he handed the photo back to me.

"Nope, I don't recall seeing any of these men down here. Sorry I can't be of more help," he said sounding sincere.

"Hey, thanks for your time and effort. I do appreciate it," I said handing him a five dollar bill in the palm of my hand so no one could see it.

The last thing you want to do is make the citizens in this end of town think you're handing out money. If they think so it's, Katie bar the door.

"Maybe Wallace will be able to put a finger on the face of one of those guys," the Frenchman said.

"I hope so. The problem with Wallace is that no one knows where he lives. I'll just have to wait until he shows up around here," I said with some discouragement reflected in my voice.

"Hey, I know where he lives," the Frenchman said, looking around to make sure he wasn't overheard.

"You do? Could you take me there? I'd like to collar this guy before he kills someone else down here."

"You and I both; come on, I'll show you."

Normally I wouldn't take off with a man down on his luck after having given him some money, especially if the man figured I had more in my wallet. The Frenchman, however, didn't pose a threat to me. After all, I wasn't under the influence of Jack, Jim, or Johnny. In fact it had been over an hour and a half since I'd given any of them a mere thought.

I asked the Frenchman how far it was to where Wallace lived and he told me it was a fair piece, so I suggested we take my car. When we got to where I'd left it the Frenchman stopped and stared at my monstrosity.

"Hey...I had a car that looked exactly like this one, except it was a Peugeot," he stated seriously.

"Then how could it look exactly like this one?"

"I meant all the dents and dings. I used to drive by the touch system. When my car touched something I knew I should stop," he laughed.

"Yeah, I've been there," I said thinking back to some of my narrow escapes.

We drove for about eight blocks before the Frenchman told me to make a left. After another four blocks he had me make another left and then a quick right. We came to a large overpass area where several freeways intersected. He told me to pull off the road and stop, which I did.

"See that tin and cardboard structure over there under the overpass," the Frenchman said pointing towards the makeshift shelter, "Well that's where Wallace hangs his hat. Be careful, though, he's got a watch dog."

"Yeah, I can see why with an estate like that," I mused.

I got out and moved cautiously in the direction of the shanty; if you could even call it that. There was a Pit Bull tied up in front of the entrance with a rope that was about ten feet long. The dog served as both a security guard and an alarm system; all the safety features a home should have.

The makeshift door was slightly ajar and I tried to look inside from a distance of eleven feet. The dog barked, growled and lunged like I was a teething bone and he wanted to sink his teeth into me. The dog's barking finally raised one of the residents inside the structure.

"Who's out there?" the man's voice said.

"It's me, Harley Quinn. I'm the guy that punched out the Chief of Police, remember?" I said hoping to jog Wallace's memory.

"Why'd you do that?" the man asked.

The question threw me. Wallace had been hip to the thought when I first met him. I had a sneaking suspicion that this was not Wallace I was talking to; when the man peeked out of the shack I saw I was right.

119

"Oh, I thought you were Wallace," I said almost apologetically.

"No, he's not here right now. He went to get us some milk for our cornflakes. We love cornflakes," the man said happily.

"The sugar frosted ones," I asked in an effort to humor the man.

"No, we're trying to cut out a lot of sugar for health reasons," the man said seriously.

I looked at the surroundings and had to smile. I guess the health craze even touches the down, down, down and out. Just as I started to say something else to the man whose face I still had not got a good look at, a voice called out from behind me. This time I recognized it as belonging to Wallace.

"Hey, what do you want?" he barked gruffly.

I looked around and saw him carrying a paper bag that I assumed contained the milk he'd gone to get. He didn't recognize me until I informed him who I was.

"Say Wallace, how goes it? I'm the guy that punched out the Chief of Police, remember?" I asked.

"Yeah, I remember...the ex-cop. What brings you down here?" he replied as he drew near.

"I have a photo I would like for you to look at and see if you recognize anyone in it as the man you saw with Blinky," I said as I unrolled the Seahawks' team photo.

"You know, I've been thinking about this and I don't want to get involved in this stuff," Wallace said shaking his head no.

"Wallace, some guy is going around killing your friends; you are involved. If he thinks you can identify him, he's going to come looking for you. I think the man that killed Conley and Blinky is the same one that ran down the Duchess, also. Now, you can go in your house there and wait for him to find you, or you can look at this photo and help me find him before he finds you," I said in an authoritative voice.

I hoped I hadn't crossed a line with Wallace, because some of the people down here are here because they hate anyone telling them what to do. In Wallace's case I was dead serious, because I knew that if the tall man he'd seen with Blinky found out he could possibly identify him, Wallace would soon wind up on a slab in the morgue.

Wallace thought about what I'd said for a moment and then looked towards the makeshift shanty.

"Yeah, I know you're right. My roommate told me I should go to the police; but you know me and my hatred for cops. You're the exception to the rule though, Quinn, because you're one of us. Let me see that photo," he said reluctantly.

I showed him the photo and he scoured the faces. Suddenly his eyes locked on one man standing to the side of the team. The man was tall, very tall. He wasn't in uniform so it didn't appear he was one of the players. I didn't know it at the time, but the man had been placed on injured reserve and had come in for the team photo shoot.

"That kind of looks like the man right there," Wallace said pointing at the man. "It's hard to say, but he sure resembles the man I saw with Blinky."

"Wallace, thank you my friend. I'll check this guy out and if he's the one we'll soon get him behind bars where he belongs," I stated.

"Why don't you just bring him down here and point him out to some of my friends; we'll save the city a lot of money," Wallace said very seriously.

"I wish I could; I really do," I agreed.

Wallace couldn't tell me anymore, but he'd given me something I could sink my teeth into by pointing out the man in the photo. I went back to the car still hearing the ferocious barking of the Pit Bull.

When I got to the car I found the Frenchman hunkered down in the front seat. I did a double take and from his crouching position he whispered loudly, "Get me out of here before Wallace sees me. If he knows I'm the one that brought you down here he'll beat the stuffing out of me...and I don't have much stuffing."

I climbed in and drove back in the direction of the rescue mission. Once we were out of sight of the overpass where Wallace called home, the Frenchman sat up and looked around with a smile on his face.

"So, did Wallace point out the guy in the photograph?" the Frenchman asked.

"He saw someone he thought might be the guy, but he couldn't be sure. I'm going to check the guy out and see what I can turn up," I replied.

"Wallace is a funny guy. I saw him beat a man up once because the guy picked a cigarette butt up off the ground and light it up. Wallace went berserk. He said it was guys like him that gave the neighborhood a bad name. Can you believe it?"

"Wallace is a pretty bad dude, huh?" I questioned.

"He can be. He fought in the Chicago Golden Gloves when he was a young man. I think he came in second or third, so he knows how to handle himself."

"I'm curious about something. Why do they call you 'the Frenchman,' because of your name?"

"Yeah, but I'll level with you if you promise to keep it to yourself," he said with a wry grin. "My name isn't really DuBonnet; that's just what I tell everyone. A lot of us down here go by different names. Take Conley for instance, you said his real name was Philpot. That doesn't surprise me. Most of us want to make it hard for any of our family to locate us, so we take on aliases.

Some just take on a nickname and that's all anyone knows them by."

"What about Blinky, was he one of the ones that just went by an alias?" I ventured.

"Yeah, but in his case it was almost given to him because of his eye condition. He'd blink like a frog in a hail storm. It was hard to watch him at times."

"How long had he had that condition, do you know?"

"From what he said, he'd gotten it about a year before he moved into our neighborhood. I think Blinky came from very good stock. Even his real name reeked of old money," the Frenchman said.

"Oh, you knew his real name?" I asked, the surprise reflected in my voice.

"Yeah, I did, but I was the only one that knew it, and he made me promise to keep it quiet! He said that some of his family had been down here looking for him. They'd found out the name of the hotel he lived in when he first moved here, so he moved to another place and took on the nickname, Blinky."

I figured I'd do a little fishing and see if I could snag something, "So Robert Waldorf told you his real name, huh?"

The Frenchman snapped his head around so quickly it's a wonder he hadn't gotten a crick in his neck. He looked at me for several moments before saying anything.

Finally he said, "Who told you that was his name? No one else down here knew that name, just me," he said firmly.

"A family member knew his name. You're right about him being from old money, he was that all right," I didn't go any further in my explanation in order to keep my client's name out of the conversation.

"I hate it when people start nosing around down here trying to find family members. I'm afraid some of my relatives will see me on television or in the newspapers and start trying to contact me. It's taken me a long time to rid myself of them so...," he stopped in mid sentence and looked at me. "I guess you've heard this all before, huh?"

"Somewhat, but it's your business, not mine."

"Thanks..., say you can let me out right up there on the corner. I see some guys I know and there's a liquor store across the street. What more could a man ask for," he laughed.

I pulled up to the curb and the Frenchman got out. Looking back in the car he smiled, "See you around, Harley," he said.

"See you Frenchman," I said and pulled back into traffic.

My next stop was the Seattle Seahawks training facilities. I wanted to put a name to the face that Wallace had put the finger on. If he was right, this could be the end of a very successful investigation that would most certainly get me some headlines, which would mean more clients. Hopefully they'd be of the class of the Philpot's and Cargill's. Only time would tell there, though.

I pulled into the visitors parking spot and got out. There were a few cars in the lot, but not a full complement seeing as how it was the player's day off. I noticed a car parked in the coach's parking spot and figured he was here. I'd heard he moved into his office on the first day of training camp and didn't leave until they'd played their last game. He was a very dedicated man.

The receptionist recognized me and buzzed the coach's office. He answered and she informed him that I wanted to talk to him. He paused before telling her to send me in.

When I opened the door I almost went into shock. The man whose picture Wallace had thought might be the man he'd seen Blinky with the night he was murdered was standing next to the coach's desk. He was definitely tall enough, standing somewhere around six feet ten or eleven inches. His long blond hair was pulled back into a pony tail and his shoulders were as wide as the front of my car.

The coach looked at me with knitted eyebrows that said 'state your case and then get out.' It would be a little hard to state my case, however, with the man in question standing within knife wielding distance from the coach. I had to play this cool. I just hoped I could pull it off.

"Hello Coach," I said.

"Quinn, what is it this time?" the coach asked.

I cast a quick glance at the mountain sized man next to the coach's desk and smiled at him; it didn't get a response one way or the other.

"I wanted to ask you about one of the men in the team photograph you gave me. I know most of the players by sight from seeing them interviewed on television or in magazines, but this one man I can't recognize," I said, wondering how I could point the man out without letting the man present know it was him I was inquiring about.

I started to hand the photo to the coach when he saved my bacon, "Oh, I'm sorry, Quinn. This is Troy Hobart. Troy is on the injured reserve list because of a knee injury. Troy, this is Harley Quinn. He's the one I told you all about in the team meeting."

I now had a name and something concrete to go on. I didn't even have to point out the man in question to the coach now. He'd given me the information without my asking. I felt a huge burden lift from my shoulders.

"Who is it you want to know about," the coach asked as he took the photo.

"Oh, this man right here," I said, pointing to the opposite side of the photo from where Troy Hobart was standing.

The coach looked at the man I was pointing to and then looked at me with a look of disdain on his face. He half closed his eyes and took a deep breath as if trying to control his temper. What had I said or done that had ticked him off, I wondered?

"That's me, Quinn," the coach said in a perturbed voice.

"It is, oh, it doesn't look anything like you," I said, trying to cover up my gaffe.

I grabbed the photo and looked at it very closely and then at the coach again.

"Oh, yeah, now I see the resemblance," I said lamely.

"Is that all you wanted to ask me, Quinn?" he asked harshly.

"Well, yes and no. I'd like to ask you a couple of very personal questions that I'm sure you do not want anyone else hearing," I said and looked at Hobart.

The coach thought for a second and then motioned towards the door of his office to the huge defensive lineman. Hobart grinned knowingly and walked to the door.

"I'll be down in the training room if you need me, Coach," Hobart said.

"Yeah, Troy, I'll be down there after a bit. Do some leg presses, but don't overdo it," the coach said.

I waited until Hobart had left before beginning my questioning of the coach.

"Coach, first of all, it wasn't you that I needed to identify; it was Troy Hobart. I didn't want to ask you his name with him standing right next to you," I explained.

The coach frowned, "Hobart? You think he might have something to do with the killings of those derelicts?" he asked.

"I have a possible identification. The eyewitness says he saw the man with one of the victims not more than an hour before the time of the murder. What I'd like to know is the whereabouts of Hobart on the nights in question; also, if he was with the team in Kansas City on the night you lost the close one at the end of the game? Can you help me out at all?"

"Troy Hobart...I find it hard to believe that he might be the killer. He's very enthusiastic about the games, but I don't think he'd kill anyone over a loss. He does take out his frustrations on the Gatorade barrel though," the coach said which jogged my memory.

"That's who it was that I saw punch the barrel on Monday Night Football," I said snapping my fingers.

"Yeah, a lot of people saw that. Hobart has really taken a ribbing about that little incident. Players can be cruel...verbally, I mean," the coach said and corrected himself quickly. He then asked me a pointed question.

"Who is it that can identify Hobart; a derelict or a...a...," he stammered.

"...A sober person," I helped him out.

"Yeah, I'd hate to think that some sot was pointing an accusing finger at one of my guys because he'd seen him on television or something," he said firmly.

"The man is quite coherent when he's sober, and he's sober more often than he's drunk. No, he'll make a reputable witness," I said knowing that it would take a major act of congress to get Wallace on a witness stand.

"I suppose he's around the rescue mission down there, huh? That's where most of them hangout," he said offhandedly.

"Well, he's there for meals, but lives about ten or eleven blocks from there under some freeway overpasses," I offered, which I shouldn't have done.

The coach looked down and shook his head.

"I was afraid it might be one of our guys. When you're in a race to the finish it's so hard not to let our emotions control us. Maybe that's what happened here, I don't know," he said thoughtfully.

"I know football fans can go over the top in their enthusiasm. You hear about some guys taking their favorite team's losses so hard they beat up their wives, girl friends, or even their own kids. I guess it isn't too big a stretch to think that a player could go off the deep end also," I stated.

"Yeah, I guess not. You have to realize that some of these guys have been coddled from the time they played high school football until they turned pro. If they're really good they get away with....well...murder. Big money is behind the games and they don't want to lose because a star player is in trouble with the law, so they buy off whomever they can. Troy Hobart isn't a star player, however. In fact, he's just about washed up as far as football goes."

I was just about to comment when the door opened and the coach's secretary looked in. He looked in her direction and raised his eyebrows as if to ask what she wanted.

"Troy said you wanted me to go down and pick up a Fed Ex delivery at the front desk, but there was no delivery there, Mr. Rawlings."

"I didn't say anything about a Fed Ex delivery," the coach said, and then looked quickly at me. "You don't suppose," he half asked.

"I'm afraid so," I said, fearing that Hobart had sent the secretary off while he listened in on our conversation.

If he had, Wallace was in danger of being another knifing victim. This time, however, it wouldn't be due to a Hawks' loss, but for silencing an eyewitness. I could have kicked myself for giving the approximate location of where Wallace lived. I had to get back down to the mission district and fast. I just hoped I wouldn't be too late.

CHAPTER

15

WHY IS IT the bigger the hurry you're in, the slower the traffic seems to move. I weaved in and out of traffic like I had on past occasions, only this time it was intentional. I got a lot of angry stares, a number of honks, and more than a few one fingered salutes; either that or people were saying the Seahawks were number one.

A fender bender stopped traffic in one lane and the other four lanes responded by instantly coming to a halt. I forced my way into the far right hand lane so I could take the next available exit and when I came to it, did just that.

This would be longer, but at least I'd be moving. I knew I'd messed up, however, when I got to the first intersection and found a road maintenance crew had a project going on that required a flagman. I love making those guys mad.

I pulled out around the four cars ahead of me and drove the shoulder up to the intersection where I could make a right turn. The problem in that was that it was a one way street going in the opposite direction. No sweat, I'd just go the wrong way for one block and then make a right and be out of harm's way.

The man in the hard hat and wearing the bright greenish yellow vest thrust his "stop" sign high in the air and when that didn't work, waved it in my direction. I nodded and smiled politely as I used the shoulder to make my illegal turn and head the wrong way.

The oncoming vehicles were no friendlier than the cars I'd gone around earlier; and knew the same sign language. I managed to make it to the corner without wrecking the wreck I was driving and found that it was a one way street going to the left instead of the right. This actually worked to my advantage, seeing as how that was the direction I wanted to go anyway.

I cut across in front of oncoming traffic and headed on towards an expressway that would put me en-route to the mission district. Traffic was even heavy on this street, but at least it was moving. I toughed out the urge to drive on the sidewalk to speed things up and finally got to the expressway on ramp. Now I could make some good time.

The old heap, I jokingly referred to as a car, had needed to have the engine blown out by really opening her up on the highway, so I figured this would be a good time to do just that. I shoved the gas pedal down and, after it slowed considerably, lurched forward as the gas fought its way through the corrosion in the car's gas line.

I know the people behind me must have thought my car was on fire, because they let me have plenty of leeway when they saw the stream of blackish/grey smoke the car belched out. I could feel the engine starting to operate better though.

Again, I weaved my way through traffic, passing cars on the left, right, and shoulder. It wasn't until I went around a patrol car that I really made good time, however. The man driving was none other than my ex-student, Carl Butterman.

I pulled to the shoulder and hopped out as Butterman exited his vehicle. When he recognized me, he shook his head negatively and tossed his ticket book back inside the vehicle.

"What's the hurry, Harley?" Butterman asked.

"I'm trying to stop a murder, and I don't mean mine. I happen to know who the killer of the derelicts is and he's on his way to silence the only witness that can place him with one of the victims. I need an escort," I said in machine gun fashion.

"Follow me; where are we going?" Butterman asked.

"Underpass city; you know the place I'm talking about; about ten blocks from the Rescue Mission," I replied.

"Let's go," Butterman said as he jumped back into his patrol car and hit the siren and gumball machine on top.

I jumped in my car and let him take the lead. His car had a lot more power than mine, but I managed to keep up with him. We covered the distance in good time. As we drew near the underpass where Wallace lived Butterman killed the siren.

I parked and jumped out, pointing in the direction of Wallace's 'residence' but didn't wait for Butterman and his partner. I ran as fast as I could, passed the other makeshift shelters until I was about forty yards from Wallace's place; that's when I stopped short.

The pit bull dog that had acted as a security guard for Wallace and his room mate was lying in a pool of blood next to the structure. The dog's throat had been cut. I drew my .45 as I neared the entrance to Wallace's domain.

The huge piece of thick cardboard that acted as a door was ajar and I could look inside the small room. I couldn't make out who it was, but someone was lying face down on the old piece of carpet used as flooring. Before I started to enter, Butterman arrived.

"Your killer has been here," he said, looking at the dog.

"He certainly has," I said and motioned inside.

Butterman drew his .9mm and quickly surveyed the area around us.

"Cover me," I said and moved inside the fancy lean to that Wallace had constructed.

The man on the warn carpet was Wallace's room mate. He had been stabbed ferociously. It was obvious that he had not died immediately, however; because written on the carpet in his own blood was the word, 'sea hawk.' Using his last bit of strength he had left an important clue. I called for Butterman to come and look at what I'd found.

"Is this the eyewitness," Butterman asked?

"No, this is his roomy. Either he got away or our killer has taken him somewhere. It's my guess that Wallace is still alive, though. The killer would have finished him here if he'd had the chance," I surmised.

"Yeah, but where did he go; that's the question?"

"I think I might know. I'll leave you to your business here, Carl. I'm heading for the rescue mission."

As I started out the door I heard Butterman say, "Drive careful."

I made it to the rescue mission in short order. When I got there I was surprised to find the doors closed and locked. This was unlike the rescue missions, to lock up in the middle of the day. That's when I saw the new Lincoln Continental parked at the end of the block. I doubted that any of this area's residence was driving something like that.

"Go Seahawks," I said when I spotted the car.

I got out and once again drew my .45 from its shoulder holster. I didn't want to run the risk of being Troy Hobart's next victim. Proceeding with great caution towards the rear of the mission, I watched for any movement around the area.

There were a lot of cardboard boxes that had been flattened, bundled, and stacked next to two large dumpsters near the back door that led to the kitchen. If I was going to lay in wait for someone that's where I would do it; if it wasn't inside the mission, that is.

I walked with my back pressed up against the building and moved towards the kitchen door that I now noticed was ajar. Maybe Hobart was still inside the mission? If he was, what was I going to find when I went in there; besides him and his knife?

As I drew near the door I heard voices coming from inside the kitchen. It was the good reverend's voice. He was talking very calmly to someone that I assumed to be Hobart.

"You don't want to do the Devil's work, son. Give me the knife and then tell me everything," the pastor said.

"I can't do that, Reverend. I'm not going to spend the rest of my life in a prison cell. Just let me take this guy with me and I'll leave the two of you alone. No one is going to miss the likes of his kind, anyway," Hobart said.

"God loves this man just as much as he loves you, or me, for that matter. God loves the sinner, but hates the sin. Now give me the knife, please," the pastor said in a kind, soft voice.

I moved up to the opened door and peeked in. I could see the pastor and Geri Munoz, but no one else. I figured that Wallace had to be hidden from my view by a large refrigerator.

Moving quietly, I crossed to the other side of the door and very slowly opened it. Hobart was so intent on the three people in front of him that he didn't notice the door opening. Once it was open wide enough that I could see where he was standing I stepped inside.

My appearing changed the situation entirely; especially since I was holding a .45 automatic in my hand. Hobart snapped his head in my direction and I saw the panic, anger, and fear in his eyes.

"Drop the knife, Hobart; it's all over," I said pointing the gun at him.

With the speed of a cornered wild cat, he threw the knife at me, hitting me in the shoulder. The razor sharp knife blade stuck deep into my shoulder causing me to inadvertently drop the gun from my hand.

Wallace broke for the door where I was standing, but Hobart was closer and cut him off. I dropped to my knees and tried to retrieve my .45. I was too late; Hobart kicked it under a large stainless steel topped table and then proceeded to kick me in the head.

All I remembered was that I saw more stars in my head than I've ever seen in the heavens on a very clear night. I lost consciousness for a few seconds, for when I regained my senses Hobart was holding Wallace in a choke hold.

Fortunately my conscious state returned quickly; something someone with my past tastes is not used to. Once I saw what was happening I rolled under the table to where my pistol lay and grabbed it up. Without even taking aim I fired at the huge hulk of a man that was bent over Wallace in preparation for snapping his neck.

The bullet hit Hobart in the side of the head, killing him instantly. He fell hard to the side and just lay there. Wallace was struggling to get to his feet, and when he finally did, ran out through the opened door and down the alleyway. The pastor hurried to Hobart and checked his pulse. There was no need; not with the left side of his head missing.

"I'm sorry I had to do that, Pastor," I said apologetically.

"You had no other choice, Mr. Quinn. He was going to kill Wallace. If you hadn't shot when you did, another two seconds would have been too late," he said and then paused before asking. "Who is he, do you know?"

"He's a football player with the Seattle Seahawks. His rage at losing close games caused him to seek out what he called 'no goods' and take out his anger over the loss on them. He killed Conley and Blinky; and he may have killed the Duchess, also," I answered.

The pastor looked at my bleeding shoulder and grabbed a clean dishtowel from a drawer and stuffed it under my shirt. While he attended to me, Geri Munoz called 911.

"Speaking of Blinky, I have some information for you about him. I learned that his real name was Robert Waldorf. At least that's what I think this means," the pastor said as he reached inside his coat and pulled out a photograph of two children.

The photo was exactly like the one Jeff Curtis had given me a copy of earlier. On the back of this one, however, were the names of the two children; Robert Waldorf and Florence Wilburn. That would be Robert Waldorf and Florence Cargill.

Once my wound had been attended to by the paramedics who arrived shortly after the police, I was told I could go; but for me to come down to police headquarters the next day and finish the necessary paper work associated with the shooting. I headed straight for my office. I wanted to inform Rodney Philpot that I'd found the killer of his brother. I hoped it would give him closure, but somehow I doubted it. It might make it a little easier, but it doesn't bring the loved one back.

Rodney, as he insisted I call him now, said he was very impressed with my work and would definitely be using my services again, as well as, recommend me to his friends. I thanked him and fought off the urge to ask him 'when.' My next call would be a little tougher.

"Hello, Mrs. Cargill, please," I said to the woman's voice on the other end of the line.

"Yes, this is she."

"Mrs. Cargill, this is Harley Quinn. I have some good news and some bad news," I said without thinking how that sounds; but it was too late to change it then.

"Oh...what is the good news?" Mrs. Cargill asked tentatively.

"I found Robert Waldorf," I said carefully.

"And the bad news," she asked.

"He's dead, Mrs. Cargill. He was murdered by the derelict killer," I said, coming straight to the point.

"Oh, no; I was afraid something might have happened to him. I'm not surprised though. That is such a terrible place to be living," she said haughtily.

"Yes, it is; but most of them choose to live like that. They love the booze more than they loved their families; even if the families are rich," I sort of agreed.

"Oh, my family wasn't rich when I was growing up, Mr. Quinn. In fact our family was poor; Robert's family was the rich one. It was through Robert's family that I met Mr. Cargill. His family was also very wealthy and I was visiting Robert when I was eighteen. That's when we met."

"I see. Well, I just wanted to let you know that you can stop the time clock. I'll give you a couple thousand dollars back, since I finished so soon," I said wanting to bite my tongue all the while.

"Oh, no; you keep the retainer that I gave you. I'm very well pleased with your work. And thank you very much, Mr. Quinn."

I said goodbye and hung up. One more call to make and then I'd get busy and drum up some more business. I wanted to tell Cassandra the good news. If I knew her, she'd want to celebrate tonight. It would be nice. I'd have to pick up a couple bottles of Martinelli's Sparkling Cider. You know, this sobriety thing could catch on. But I had a sneaking suspicion I was getting hooked on sparkling cider.

CHAPTER

16

CASSANDRA SMILED as she dished up the mashed potatoes. I poured us each a glass of sparkling cider and waited for her to bring the sizzling steaks from the kitchen.

"So Mrs. Cargill seemed to be all right with her cousin being murdered?" she asked.

"Yeah, she took it very well. But, why shouldn't she? It had been years since they'd seen each other. I really didn't find out that much about him. She could only tell me things about their childhood. In fact, she didn't even tell me that her family had been very poor when she was growing up."

"I don't know why, Cass, but something doesn't sit right about this case with Blinky. Don't ask me to explain it right now, because I can't. But, there's something not right."

"Like what?"

"Why all of a sudden does Mrs. Cargill decide to locate her long lost cousin? Why hadn't she made more attempts to do so earlier? And why would Rodney Philpot be talking to his high society friends about hiring an alcoholic ex-cop to try to find the killer of his brother? No, something's wrong."

Cassandra grew silent, studious even. I could tell something was on her mind. I knew she'd tell me what it was, though.

"It seems like I just read something about the Cargill's in the paper recently. I didn't really read the story, because it was before they had hired you. Let's see, when was that, anyway?" Cass pondered.

"I only worked for them for about three days, if that helps?"

"It does...in fact I'll bet I still have the article in that stack of old papers over there," Cass said as she pointed towards a magazine holder next to her recliner.

"Was it in the society section," I asked?

"No, I don't think so. Look in the local news portion of the paper; that's where I saw it."

I got up and walked over to where she kept the papers. Thumbing through them I found the article quickly enough. I began reading and found myself totally absorbed after reading just the first sentence. The article was about the Waldorf inheritance being held up in probate due to no one being able to locate the only heir to the Waldorf fortune; their son, Robert.

As I continued to read I saw something that really got my juices to flowing. The next heir in line was Mrs. Florence Cargill, a first cousin. The inheritance was said to be in excess of nine hundred million dollars. I suddenly had a thought run through my brain that really got me to thinking.

As I thought back to things that had been said, something kept trying to push its way through to the front of the thought process line. I focused on that one thought and let it develop. It was a question; but a big one.

Something that Rodney Philpot had said suddenly glowed like a candle on a moonless night. He'd said he would recommend me to some of his friends. I thought he already had been recommending me to his friends; at least that was the impression I'd gotten from Mrs. Cargill.

The bad feeling continued to grow but I still didn't know why. My first thoughts were that since the Cargill's were in the process of inheriting almost a billion dollars they needed proof that Robert Waldorf, better known as 'Blinky', was indeed one of the victims of the killer.

Then my thoughts really went haywire. What if I'd been wrong about the motives of the killings all along? What if the murders were only made to look like they coincided with the losses of the Seahawks so the police would be looking for a serial killer that was a football fanatic?

Cassandra brought the two steaks in on a platter and set them down on the table. When she looked at my face she knew something wasn't right.

"What is it, Harley?" she asked.

"I'm not sure, Cass. I might have been totally wrong on this whole case. I think I've been following a false lead that still managed to get me to the killer. The motive behind the killings very well could have been money. This is what the article in the newspaper said," I stated and read the article to Cass.

When I'd finished she stared at me with a very serious look on her face.

"You're not suggesting that the Cargill's hired this Hobart to kill her cousin are you? Because if you are, Harley, you'd better tread very lightly. These people are so far above the upper crust that the upper crust is the bottom of the loaf."

"I know, I know; but look at it? When you put nearly a billion dollar price on someone's head they become expendable. I'll never forget the words of John D. Rockefeller when asked how much was enough money?

141

He answered, 'Just a little bit more.' I guarantee the Cargill's would answer the same way."

"How are you going to prove it?" Cass asked.

"I'm going to break the law by doing a little breaking and entering and take a look around Hobart's home. If he was hired by the Cargill's to kill Blinky I might run across something in his personal belongings. I've got to see if I can connect Hobart to Mr. or Mrs. Cargill. And I'm thinking, Mrs. Cargill."

"I hope you're not getting in too deep, Harley? This could be very dangerous," Cass warned.

"Now you know why my first wife couldn't live with me...well that and my friends; Jack, Jim, and Johnny."

"When are you going to check out his house...tonight?" Cass asked.

"Yes, as soon as possible; but I'll wait until it's good and dark."

"Well, you're not going to go before you eat dinner," Cass said with a smile.

"That's right, Ollie," I said in my best Stan Laurel voice, and made the face and gesture of scratching my head ala Stanley.

Cass seemed to be worried about my attempting to connect the Cargill's to the murder of Robert Waldorf, a.k.a. Blinky. She looked beautiful as she peered across the dining room table at me. I could see the worry in her beautiful eyes. I was one lucky man to have a woman like her worrying about me; and a woman that could cook like her.

Dinner was delicious.

It was close to twelve thirty in the morning when I parked next to Troy Hobart's home. I looked around to make sure no one was watching as I slipped over the six foot high fence that surrounded Hobart's home. His place wasn't elaborate, but spacious with a nice piece of land that was nicely manicured. The house was spread out, having a total of twelve rooms, not counting bathrooms.

I didn't figure there would be a security alarm system set, since he was dead. I checked though before breaking the window in a back bedroom and climbing through. Fortunately, Hobart had the halls lighted with automatic nightlights so it made getting around very easy.

Walking down the hallway and checking each room I'd almost reached the huge living room when I opened a door to Hobart's office. I could tell the room had been gone over by the police. They were looking for one particular kind of clues, but I was now looking for another kind of clue.

I went through his desk and found nothing of interest. The large file cabinet might be a better source of information, I hoped. Nothing there. Then I thought of a wall safe. I checked the different paintings hanging on the walls and noticed that none of them were askew. This indicated to me that the police had not even looked to see if there was a wall safe, or not.

The second painting yielded me my prize. The wall safe was easy enough for me to crack, seeing as how I had attended several workshops the police had us go through on breaking and entering. I finished at the top of my class I might add. I could have been a cat burglar; but who wants to rob cats?

Mr. Hobart was taking no chances that the ones that hired him would try and double cross him. He had an entire scenario written as to how he would go about setting up a false trail for the police to follow. He figured that since this was Seattle the police would readily connect the dots to the win, loss column of the Hawk's football season. Little did he know that his own fanaticism would direct attention to him.

Mr. Hobart even had the names of the principles in the murder plot. I read the names aloud.

"Mr. Norval Cargill, Mrs. Florence Cargill, Mr. Gaylord Brancifort, and Miss X; hmm, I wonder who Brancifort and Miss X are?"

"Brancifort would be me, Mr. Quinn," the voice said from behind me.

I whirled around to find myself staring down the business end of a .9 mm automatic. The gun looked as big as the man holding it, not that he was a lightweight; it was just that a gun always looks bigger when it's aimed at you.

"That still leaves the question, who are you?" I asked again.

"Actually, I'm the Cargill's attorney. You see, Mr. Quinn, in order for Mrs. Cargill to inherit the nine hundred and ninety four million dollars her cousin, the late Mr. Waldorf, had to be dead. Well, guess what; he is! Of course we had to arrange his demise. Now it appears that we'll have to arrange yours," the man dapperly dressed said.

"I have another question for you before you pull that trigger. How'd you come to know Troy Hobart? I can't picture you being a football fan?"

"I represented him in an assault and battery case some time ago and learned that the man had absolutely no conscience. He'd do anything if the price was right. We offered him five million dollars to kill Waldorf and he went for it."

"So why did Mrs. Cargill hire me to find her cousin if you knew he was dead?"

"That was my idea. We'd let you settle the probate problem by discovering that 'Blinky' was actually Robert Waldorf. Clever, don't you think?"

"I have one more question. How'd you know I was coming out here? I doubt that you just happened to drop in."

"We figured you'd be showing up here sooner or later; if you were half the detective we were told you were. And it helped to receive a phone call about your intentions."

"So you had someone watching me, huh? I'm flattered," I said with a crooked grin.

I've always been the kind of guy that likes to take the bull by the horns when I'm working on a case; a case of anything. I had the bull by the horns now, but the problem was it was dragging me all over the cow pasture. I didn't know how I was going to get myself extricated from this mess.

Just as I was about to say something else very witty, or stupid, I caught the slight movement of someone in the doorway to the room. I couldn't make out who it was, only that it was a woman. My heart broke and my ideals shattered when they hit the cold hard facts of reality.

I looked at the silhouette and spoke, "Come on out, Cass," I said.

The woman stood motionless at first, but after a few seconds slowly moved into full view. My world suddenly turned very dark and cold as I peered into the beautiful face of the woman that had been my lover, best friend, and confidant. I wanted to throw up and scream all at the same time, but did neither.

"How'd you know, Harley?" Cassandra asked with a questioning in her voice.

"How else would Bozo here have known I was coming out here? It had to be someone that knew of my intentions and you were the only one that knew. Why...and how did you get involved with these people?"

"The Cargill's are major stockholders in the company I work for and they found out that you and I was an item. When Gaylord approached me with an offer of two million dollars to let them know what you found out about Robert Waldorf, I couldn't refuse," she said as she moved over next to Brancifort.

"So you sold me out. Well, at least I'm worth two million to you. Are you going to be present when *'Gaylord'* here, pulls the trigger? Maybe they should have you do it to insure your silence? Otherwise you could always go to the police and feign ignorance as to what they were plotting," I said, more or less attempting to keep the conversation going, and thus, stalling for more time.

My suggestion found a home with Brancifort because he glanced at Cassandra as though considering it. The slight distraction was all I needed. I didn't waste any time diving for cover behind the desk that was about seven feet from where I was standing.

Brancifort fired wildly as I dived for cover, the bullet just nicking me in the calf of my leg. It burned like fire, but not enough to slow me down. I grabbed my .45 and fired five shots in rapid succession; just my hand sticking above the desk top. If nothing else it would send the two of them running for cover.

Obviously Brancifort was new to the crime of murder. He hadn't even taken the time to relieve me of my weapon; something anyone that had perpetrated a crime, or had any common sense at all would have done first off.

Another shot rang out from Brancifort's gun, but the bullet went straight down into the floor. His body followed shortly afterwards. I'd hit him with two of the slugs with which I'd sprayed the room. I'd also hit someone else; Cassandra.

When I looked cautiously over the top of the desk I saw her. She was in a sitting position with her back against the doorpost. I could tell she was hurt badly by the blank, wide eyed stare on her face. She slowly looked in my direction and held out her hand as if pleading for help. That was the last time she ever reached out to me. I hurried to her, but it was too late. Just as I reached her, her head dropped forward and she slowly slumped to the floor.

As I stood there in the semi-darkness looking down at the woman I'd loved so much, I could hear the distant wailing of sirens. Obviously I been wrong about the place not having a security alarm system hooked up since Hobart was dead. All I could do was stand and wait...and remember.

Life is a journey that keeps a person on their toes constantly. Every day we live is a new page in an ever growing novel of life. When we reach the end of one chapter another chapter, a new one, is started. Cassandra had been a bright spot in the chapter that had just ended. I'd miss her not being in my life's story anymore. I guess her love for money was stronger than her love for me. Love can make people do some very strange things. What is it the Bible says? Oh, yeah. 'For the love of money is the root of all evil'...and, you can add, a motive for murder.

The End

Other Books by This Author
(In alphabetical order)

**8 Seconds to Glory
Aces and Eights
A Walk on the Wilder Side
Beyond Missing
Brimstone; End of the Trail
Brotherhood of the Cobra
Corrigan; Proud to Serve
Day of the Rawhiders
Four Corners Woman
In the Chill of the Night
Last of the Long Riders
Night of the Blood Red Moon
Return to Cutter's Creek
Ride the Hellfire Trail
The Long Ride Back
The Woman in the Field
The Mystery of Myrtle Creek
Yellow Sky, Black Hawk**